3o min~knits

30 min~knits

what can you knit in half an hour or less?

carol meldrum

A QUINTET BOOK

First edition for the United States and Canada
published in 2012 by Barron's Educational Series, Inc.

All inquiries should be addressed to:
Barron's Educational Series, Inc.
250 Wireless Boulevard
Hauppauge, NY 11788
www.barronseduc.com

Library of Congress Control Number: 2011946189

ISBN: 978-1-4380-0129-6

QTT.TMK

Conceived, designed, and produced by
Quintet Publishing Limited
The Old Brewery
6 Blundell Street
London N7 9BH
UK

Project Editor: Alison Hissey
Designer: Simon Daley
Additional Design: Jane Laurie and Rod Teasdale
Copyeditor: Liz Jones
Illustrators: Bernard Chau and Jane Laurie
Art Director: Michael Charles
Editorial Director: Donna Gregory
Publisher: Mark Searle

Printed in China by 1010 Printing International Limited

9 8 7 6 5 4 3 2 1

contents

65 00035 4052

introduction

Think you're too busy to knit anything? Think again! Here's a collection of knitting projects that you really can fit into your spare time. Be inspired to pick up your needles, dip into this fantastic book, and get knitting.

Each pattern has been designed to let you see results fast—you'll be surprised at just how much you can create in half-hour pockets of time throughout the day. Even better, they can all be knitted from those little scraps of yarn left over from other projects.

The book includes full instructions covering all of the techniques used in the patterns, so it's a perfect place to start if you are new to knitting and looking to extend your skills. For the more experienced knitter there is also a mix of slightly more advanced techniques to keep you interested throughout. Colored tabs throughout the book show good patterns for practicing particular skills.

With such a wide variety of projects at your fingertips, you will keep coming back to this collection—whether for last-minute gift ideas or simply to satisfy an urge to create, there is something for everyone.

A NOTE ABOUT TIME

All of the knits are achievable in a 30-minute time slot, but this will depend on your basic knitting speed and familiarity with the techniques used in the pattern. The making up and adding of the finishing touches to the projects is not included in the 30 minutes. Also, where a project is made up of more than one item (such as the fingerless gloves, see page 45), knitting a single item can be achieved in 30 minutes, but knitting all of the items for the project may take longer.

For faster results, there are a few tips and techniques that will help you on your way:

• Have a quick read through the pattern instructions to see what's involved before casting on.

• Gather all your equipment and materials before you start—yarn, needles, scissors, and tape measure if necessary.

• Most importantly, relax! Don't worry too much about the exact time a project will take—it's not a race.

project selector

easy projects

chick
page 11

egg
page 12

egg cozy
page 13

fish
page 14

mug cozy
page 15

coasters
page 17

potholder
page 18

napkin rings
page 19

little birds
page 21

apple pincushion
page 22

golden pear
page 24

phone cover
page 26

pencil case
page 27

baby pixie hat
page 29

strawberry beanie
page 30

teddy bear baby hat
page 32

tiny kitty
page 33

tiny teddy
page 34

rib lace pompom hat
page 37

ladybug key ring
page 38

bumblebee key ring
page 39

ear warmer
page 41

arm warmers
page 42

bracelet
page 43

fingerless gloves
page 45

button neck warmer
page 46

lampshade decoration
page 49

wrist corsage
page 50

scented heart
page 51

picture frames
page 52

finger puppets
page 55

coin purse
page 57

Dalí mustache
page 58

bow hairpins
page 60

crown
page 61

catnip mouse
page 62

flower hairband
page 63

covered hairclip
page 65

bunting
page 67

small cat pillow
page 68

intermediate projects

lion
page 69

broad strap booties
page 70

sheep magnet
page 72

crossover booties
page 73

baby mittens
page 75

Venetian mask
page 77

leaf headband
page 80

flowers
page 82

strawberry charm
page 86

tea light decorations
page 87

cable coat hanger
page 88

knitted collar
page 89

crossover scarf
page 90

string of birds
page 93

acorn
page 95

tumbling leaves
page 96

dog bone key ring
page 98

dragonfly
page 99

butterfly clip
page 100

Aztec pot cover
page 102

chick

Which came first, the chick or the egg? In this case, it depends which one you knit first! This novelty design is so cute, made up of two different-sized basic ball shapes stitched together—and with the addition of wings, beak, and eyes the chick's ready to go.

BODY

Using size US 6 (4 mm) needles, cast on 10 sts.

Row 1 (WS): Purl to end.

Row 2: K1, * M1 by picking up the strand in between stitches and knitting into the back, K1, rep to last st, K1 (18 sts).

Row 3: Purl to end.

Row 4: K2, * M1, K2, rep from * to end (26 sts).

Starting with a purl row work 11 rows in stockinette stitch.

Row 16: K2, K2tog, * K1, K2tog, rep from * to last st, K1 (18 sts).

Row 17: Purl to end.

Row 18: K1, * K2tog, rep from * to last st, k1 (10 sts).

Row 19: Purl to end.

Break off yarn, leaving a good length for sewing up, thread through 10 sts on needle, pull tight, and secure. Using same length of yarn, sew seam toward cast-on edge.

HEAD

Using size US 6 (4 mm) needles, cast on 10 sts.

Row 1 (WS): Purl to end.

Row 2: K1, * M1 by picking up the strand in between stitches and knitting into the back, K1, rep to last st, K1. (18 sts).

Starting with a purl row work 7 rows in stockinette stitch.

Row 10: K1, * K2tog, rep from * to last st, K1 (10 sts).

Row 11: Purl to end.

Break off yarn, leaving a good length, thread through 10 sts on needle, pull tight, and secure. Using same length of yarn sew seam toward cast-on edge.

ASSEMBLY

Insert stuffing from the bottom opening of both the head and the body. Once you are happy with the shape, sew up the bottom opening.

MATERIALS

Rowan Creative Focus Worsted (75% wool, 25% alpaca, approx. 220 yd/ 200 m per 3½ oz/100 g ball) 1 x shade 3810 Saffron

Toy stuffing

Black thread

½-in (1-cm) square orange felt fabric for beak

Orange thread

2 small shirt buttons for eyes

EQUIPMENT

1 pair size US 6 (4 mm) knitting needles

Tapestry needle

Sharp sewing needle

GAUGE

Approx. 22 sts x 30 rows = 4 in (10 cm) in stockinette stitch

◄ projects

Position the bottom of the head on the top of the body and sew into position.

WINGS *make 2*

Using size US 6 (4 mm) needles, cast on 3 sts.
Row 1 (WS): K1, P1, K1.
Row 2: K1, M1, K1, M1, K1 (5 sts).
Row 3: Knit to end.
Row 4: K1, P3, K1.
Repeat the last 2 rows once more.
Next row: K1, Sl2 knitwise, K1, p2sso, K1 (3 sts).
Next row: K1, P1, K1.
Next row: K3tog.
Break off yarn and thread through last sts.

Block and press wings.
Using picture as guide, pin and stitch into position on body of chick.

FINISHING

Cut a small square out of orange felt fabric. Fold in half to create a triangle. Next pin and stitch onto front of head in the desired position.
Attach the eyes to sides of head.

egg

This fun egg pattern is a great way to practice your increasing and decreasing skills. Why not add a few stripes, or add a loop to the top to make a perfect decoration?

Using size US 3 (3.25 mm) needles, cast on 10 sts.
Row 1 (WS): Purl to end.
Row 2: K1, * M1 by picking up the strand in between stitches and knitting into the back, K1, rep to end (19 sts).
Row 3: Purl to end.
Row 4: K3, * M1, K2, rep from * to last 3 sts, M1, K1 (26 sts).
Starting with a purl row, work 15 rows in stockinette stitch.
Row 20: K2, K2tog, * K1, K2tog, rep from * to last st, K1 (18 sts).

Starting with a purl row, work 3 rows in stockinette stitch.
Row 24: K1, * K2tog, rep from * to last st, k1 (10 sts).
Row 25: Purl to end.
Break off yarn, leaving a good length for sewing up, thread through 10 sts on needle, pull tight, and secure. Using same length of yarn, sew seam toward cast-on edge.
Insert stuffing from the bottom opening. Once you are happy with the shape, sew up the bottom opening.

MATERIALS

Rowan Pure Life Organic Cotton DK (100% cotton, approx. 131 yd/120 m per 1¾ oz/50g ball)
1 x shade 989 Cherry plum

Toy stuffing

EQUIPMENT

1 pair size US 3 (3.25 mm) knitting needles
Tapestry needle

GAUGE

Approx. 26 sts x 33 rows = 4 in (10 cm) in stockinette stitch

egg cozy

Keep your boiled eggs nice and warm with this cute cozy design. Inspired by traditional Cornish pottery, the cozy is worked in a classic blue-and-white stripe. The fabric is a simple rib and is given an extra twist with the introduction of a cable.

Using size US 6 (4 mm) needles and yarn A, cast on 32 sts.

Row 1: P2, * K4, P2, rep from * to end.

Row 2: K2, * P4, K2, rep from * to end.

Change to yarn B—do not break off yarn A.

Row 3: Repeat row 1.

Row 4: Repeat row 2.

Row 5: P2, * C4B, P2, rep from * to end.

Row 6: Repeat row 2.

The last 6 rows form the pattern.

Keeping the stripe pattern correct (2 rows yarn A followed by 4 rows yarn B), repeat rows 1–6 once more then rows 1–4 once more.

Change to yarn B.

Row 17: P2, * K2togtbl, K2tog, P2, rep from * to end (22 sts).

Row 18: K2, * P2, K2, rep from * to end.

Row 19: P2, * K2tog, P2, rep from * to end (17 sts).

Row 20: K2, * P1, K2, rep from * to end.

Break off yarn leaving a good length, then thread through the sts on needle.

ASSEMBLY

Pull tight yarn that the stitches are on and secure. Then using the same length of yarn, sew the side seams together.

FINISHING

Using approx. 24 in (60 cm) of yarn A make twisted cord for loop at top of cozy.

Thread the non-knotted end of the twisted cord through tapestry needle. Bring the needle up through the top of the cozy, and then back down.

Turn the cozy inside out and knot the ends of the loop together.

MATERIALS

Rowan Kid Classic (70% lambswool, 22% kid mohair, 8% polymide, approx. 153 yd/140 m per 1¾ oz/ 50 g ball)
A shade 873 Deep blue
B shade 828 Feather

EQUIPMENT

1 pair size US 6 (4 mm) knitting needles
Tapestry needle

GAUGE

Approx. 22 sts x 30 rows = 4 in (10 cm) in stockinette stitch

FINISHED SIZE

To fit average egg

fish

These fun stripy fish are the perfect way to practice all of your knitting skills. The shape is created using a mixture of increasing and decreasing techniques in stockinette stitch throughout. The front and back are knitted at the same time so minimal sewing is required.

MATERIALS

Patons 100% mercerized cotton DK (approx. 230 yd/210 m per ball)
A shade 2729 Delta
B shade 2691 White
C shade 2115 Red
D shade 2739 Kingfisher

2 x ½-in (1-cm) buttons per fish

Polyester toy filling

EQUIPMENT

1 pair size US 3 (3.25 mm) knitting needles

Tapestry needle

PATTERN

Each fish is knitted to the same basic pattern but has its own stripe sequence—follow the pattern and stripe sequence for the desired fish.

BASIC FISH

Using size US 3 (3.25 mm) needles, cast on 28 sts.

Work 1 row of purl as foundation row.

Row 1: K2, * K2togtbl, K3, M1 by picking up the strand in between stitches and knit into the back, K1, M1, K3, K2tog, K2, rep from * once more to end.

Row 2: Purl to end.

Row 3: K2, * K3togtbl, K2, M1, K1, M1, K2, K3tog, K2, rep from * once more to end (24 sts).

Row 4: Purl to end.

Row 5: K2, * K3togtbl, K1, M1, K1, M1, K1, K3tog, K2, rep from * once more to end (20 sts).

Row 6: Purl to end.

Row 7: K2, * K3togtbl, M1, K1, M1, K3tog, K2, rep from * once more to end (16 sts).

Starting with a purl row, work 9 rows in stockinette stitch.

Row 17: K4, M1, K1, M1, K6, M1, K1, M1, K4 (20 sts).

Starting with a purl row, work 5 rows in stockinette stitch.

Row 23: K5, M1, K1, M1, K8, M1, K1, M1, K5 (24 sts).

Starting with a purl row, work 3 rows in stockinette stitch.

Row 27: K4, K2togtbl, K1, K2tog, K6, K2togtbl, K1, K2tog, K4 (20 sts).

Starting with a purl row, work 5 rows in stockinette stitch.

Row 33: K3, K2togtbl, K1, K2tog, K4, K2togtbl, K1, K2tog, K3 (16 sts).

Starting with a purl row, work 3 rows in stockinette stitch.

Row 37: K2, K2togtbl, K1, K2tog, K2, K2togtbl, K1, K2tog, K2 (12 sts).

Row 38: Purl to end.

Row 39: K1, Sl1, K2tog, psso K4, Sl1, K2tog, psso, K1 (8sts).

Leaving a long enough length to sew up side seam, break off yarn and thread through 8sts on needle. Pull tight to secure.

ASSEMBLY

Weave in loose ends, and then gently press on the wrong side with a steam iron.

Next sew up side seam using mattress stitch, using length left earlier. Sew, working down toward the tail and making sure that the stripes match up. Leave the tail open and insert stuffing. Once you are happy with stuffing, sew up tail.

Next sew button to head using contrast yarn.

FISH A STRIPE

Cast on in yarn A.
Rows 1–32: Yarn A.
Rows 33–34: Yarn C.
Rows 35 to end: Yarn B.

FISH B STRIPE

Cast on in yarn A.
Rows 1–4: Yarn A.
Rows 5–8: Yarn D.
Rows 9–12: Yarn A.
Rows 13–16: Yarn D.
Rows 17–20: Yarn A.
Rows 21–24: Yarn D.
Rows 25–28: Yarn A.
Rows 29–32: Yarn D.
Rows 33 to end: Yarn B.

FISH C STRIPE

Cast on in yarn C.
Rows 1–2: Yarn C.
Rows 3–6: Yarn B.
Rows 7–8: Yarn C.
Rows 9–12: Yarn B.
Rows 13–14: Yarn C.
Rows 15–18: Yarn B.
Rows 19–20: Yarn C.
Rows 21–24: Yarn B.
Rows 25–26: Yarn C.
Rows 27–30: Yarn B.
Rows 31–32: Yarn C.
Rows 33 to end: Yarn D.

mug cozy

This mug cozy not only looks good, but will help keep your coffee nice and hot. The rib fabric ensures that one size fits all, and the button fastening to the side makes space for the handle.

Using size US 8 (5 mm) needles and yarn A, cast on 38 sts.
Row 1: K2, * P2, K2, rep from * to end.
Row 2: P2, * K2, P2, rep from * to end.
Row 3: K2, * P2, K2, rep to last 4 sts, P1, yo, K2tog, K1.
Row 4: Repeat row 2.
Change to yarn B.
Work as rows 1 and 2 twice more. The last 8 rows form pattern repeat.
Keeping stripe sequence correct work last 8 rows once more then rows 1–4 once more.
Bind off loosely in rib.

Tip: If you bind off tightly, use a size US 9 (5.5 mm) needle to bind off.
Weave in loose ends.
Do not press as you will flatten the rib.
Match up buttons to buttonholes and sew into position, use a contrast yarn if desired—here Rowan Cotton Glace shade 741 Poppy was used.

RIBBING

MATERIALS

Rowan Kid Classic (70% lambswool, 22% kid mohair, 8% polymide, approx. 153 yd/140 m per 1¾ oz/ 50 g ball)
A shade 873 Deep blue
B shade 828 Feather

3 four-hole buttons approx. ¾ in (1.5 cm) diameter

EQUIPMENT

1 pair size US 8 (5 mm) knitting needles

GAUGE

Approx. 19 sts x 25 rows = 4 in (10 cm) in stockinette stitch

FINISHED SIZE

To fit standard mug

coasters

These circular coasters will brighten up any table—working from the outer edge you simply decrease all the way. Knitted in brightly colored 100 percent cotton they can be popped into the washing machine, making them pretty yet practical. Each coaster is decorated with a different floral motif.

MATERIALS

Rowan Handknit cotton DK (100% cotton, approx. 93 yd/85 m per 1¾ oz/ 50g ball)
A shade 349 Ochre
B shade 352 Sea foam
C shade 215 Rosso
D shade 219 Gooseberry

Selection of colors of cotton yarn for embroidery (e.g. red, dark green, olive green, lime green)

EQUIPMENT

1 pair size US 3 (3.25 mm) knitting needles

Tapestry needle

Embroidery needle

Work 1 coaster in each of the colors as follows:

Using size US 3 (3.25 mm) needles cast on 74 sts.

Row 1: Purl to end.

Row 2: K7 * K2togtbl, K6, rep from * to last 3 sts, K2togtbl, K1 (65 sts).

Row 3: Purl to end.

Row 4: K6, * K2togtbl, K5, rep from * to last 3 sts, K2togtbl K1 (56 sts).

Row 5: Purl to end.

Row 6: K5, * K2togtbl, K4, rep from * to last 3 sts, K2togtbl K1 (47 sts).

Row 7: Purl to end.

Row 8: K4, * K2togtbl, K3, rep from * to last 3 sts, K2togtbl K1 (38 sts).

Row 9: Purl to end.

Row 10: K3, * K2togtbl, K2, rep from * to last 3 sts, K2togtbl K1 (29 sts).

Row 11: Purl to end.

Row 12: K2, * K2togtbl, K1, rep from * to last 3 sts, K2togtbl K1 (20 sts).

Row 13: Purl to end.

Row 14: K1, * K2togtbl, rep from * to last 3 sts, K2togtbl K1 (11 sts).

Row 15: Purl to end.

Break off yarn leaving long enough length to sew seam. Pull yarn through remaining stitches.

ASSEMBLY

Using length of yarn, sew seams together using mattress stitch technique.

Weave in loose ends on wrong side of fabric.

Block and press to flatten fabric and seam.

EMBROIDERY

Using picture as guide, embroider flower embellishments onto the front of the coaster.

Coaster A: Work 4 daisy stitches in red for petals, backstitch in dark green for stem and daisy stitch in dark green for leaves.

◄ projects

Coaster B: Work French knot for center of flower, then in contrast color work satin stitch in 3 sections around French knot for petals, then work bullion stitches around petals for leaves in olive green.

Coaster C: Work 5 bullion stitches as petals in ecru, 3 French knots at center in turquoise, fly stitch as stem in lime green.

Coaster D: Work 5 daisy stitch petals in a circle for petals, then work French knot at center, work stem as given for coaster A.

potholder

This pattern is perfect if you are new to knitting. It's a great way to practice your knit and purl stitches and make a practical project. The potholder is knitted in a cotton and polyamide blend fisherman-weight yarn with a rounded appearance that really makes the checkerboard pattern stand out. It also makes a great washcloth.

Using size US 7 (4.5 mm) needles, cast on 32 sts.

Row 1: *K4, P4, rep from * to end.

Row 2: Repeat row 1.

Repeat rows 1–2 once more.

Row 5: * P4, K4, rep from * to end.

Row 6: Repeat row 5.

Repeat rows 5–6 once more.

The last 8 rows form the pattern. Repeat 3 more times, then repeat rows 1–4 once more.

Bind off.

FINISHING

Weave in all the loose ends, then pin out into a square and gently press.

MATERIALS

Rowan All Seasons Cotton (60% cotton, 40% acrylic, approx. 99 yd/90 m per 1¾ oz/50 g ball)
1 x shade 178 Organic

EQUIPMENT

1 pair size US 7 (4.5 mm) knitting needles

GAUGE

Approx. 25 sts x 18 rows = 4 in (10 cm) in stockinette stitch

napkin rings

These woven-effect napkin rings will match perfectly with the coasters (see page 17). Match up the colors and embroidery stitches to create a stunning tableware set.

Using yarn A, B, or C and size US 3 (3.25 mm) needles, cast on 10 sts.

Change to size US 6 (4 mm) needles.

Row 1 (RS): K1, * Sl1, K1, psso but instead of dropping slipped stitch from left-hand needle, knit into the back of it, rep from * to last stitch, K1.

Row 2: * P2tog, then purl 1st stitch again slipping both stitches off the needle together, rep from * to end.

The last 2 rows form pattern. Repeat these 2 rows until work measures approx. 4 in (10 cm) ending with a purl row.

Bind off using size US 3 (3.25 mm) needles.

Block and press.

Sew cast-on and bound-off edges together to form ring.

EMBROIDERY

Using picture as guide, embroider flower embellishments onto the front of the napkin rings.

Ring A: Work 4 daisy stitches in red for petals, backstitch in dark green for stem, and daisy stitch in dark green for petals.

Ring B: Work French knot for center of flower, then in contrast color work satin stitch in 3 sections around French knot for petals, then work bullion stitches around petals for leaves in olive green.

Ring C: Work 5 bullion stitches as petals in ecru, 3 French knots at center in turquoise, and fly stitch as stem in lime green.

Ring D: Work 5 daisy stitch petals in a circle for petals, then work French knot at center, and work stem as given for ring A.

MATERIALS
Rowan Handknit Cotton DK (100% cotton, approx. 93 yd/85 m per 1³⁄₄ oz/ 50g ball)

A shade 349 Ochre
B shade 352 Sea foam
C shade 215 Rosso
D shade 219 Gooseberry

Selection of colors of cotton yarn for embroidery

EQUIPMENT

1 pair size US 6 (4 mm) knitting needles

1 pair size US 3 (3.25 mm) knitting needles

Tapestry needle

Embroidery needle

little birds

These tiny birds are so simple and quick to make, and just perfect for using up any spare scraps of yarn and felt fabric you have in your collection.

BODY
Using size US 2 (2.75 mm) needles, cast on 6 sts.
Row 1: Purl.
Row 2: KFB in every stitch (12 sts).
Row 3: Purl.
Row 4: KFB in every stitch (24 sts).
Row 5: Purl.
Row 6: *K1, KFB* repeat across (36 sts).
Row 7: Purl.
Row 8: Knit.
Row 9: Purl.
Row 10: *K1, K2tog* across (24 sts).
Row 11: Purl.
Row 12: *K1, K2tog* (16 sts).
Row 13: Purl.
Row 14: Knit.
Row 15: Purl.
Row 16: (K2tog) to end (8 sts).
Row 17: (P2tog) to end (4 sts).
Cut yarn leaving 8 in (20 cm) tail, run thread through remaining stitches, and pull gently.

WINGS *make 2*
With main color (MC), cast on 8 stitches on size US 2 (2.75 mm) needles.
Row 1: Knit 1 row.
Row 2: P1, P2tog, P2, P2tog, P1 (6 sts).
Row 3: With contrast color (CC), knit.
Row 4: Purl.
Row 5: With MC, K1, K2tog, K2tog, K1 (4 sts).
Row 6: Purl.
Row 7: With CC, K2tog, K2tog (2 sts).
Row 8: P2tog (1 st).
Cut yarn and run thread through remaining stitches to close.

ASSEMBLY
Using tapestry needle, sew halfway up the back of the body piece using mattress stitch. Sew eyes in place, then stuff the body before finishing seaming.
Sew the wings to the body along the long cast-on edge.
Cut a small diamond shape from yellow felt and sew in place by neatly stitching across the center (widest part). Dab a small amount of glue on either side of the stitching and pinch the beak closed until it holds its shape.
Finally, sew a loop of yarn to the head of the bird for hanging.

apple pincushion

This pattern is a modern take on the classic tomato pincushion. The shape is created using increasing and decreasing techniques, and the fabric is then hand felted so your needles and pins won't disappear into the cushion. Decorated with a stalk and leaf motif to add a touch of character, this sweet design will be a welcome addition to your sewing kit.

Using size US 7 (4.5 mm) needles, cast on 11 sts.

Row 1 (WS): Purl to end.

Row 2: K1, *M1 by picking up the strand in between stitches and knitting into the back, K1, repeat from * to last st, K1 (20 sts).

Row 3: Purl to end.

Row 4: K1, M1, K2, rep from * to last st, K1 (29 sts).

Row 5: Purl to end.

Row 6: K1, M1, K3, rep from * to last st, K1 (38 sts).

Row 7: Purl to end.

Row 8: K1, M1, K4, rep from * to last st, K1 (47 sts).

Starting with a purl row, work in stockinette stitch for 9 rows.

Row 18: K1, * K2tog, K3, rep from * to last st, K1 (38 sts).

Row 19: Purl to end.

Row 20: K1, * K2tog, K2, rep from * to last st, K1 (29 sts).

Row 21: Purl to end.

Row 22: K1, * K2tog, K1, rep from * to last st, K1 (20 sts).

Row 23: Purl to end.

Row 24: K1, * K2tog, rep from * to last st, K1 (11 sts).

Break off yarn leaving a good length, thread through 11 sts on needle and pull tight, then secure.

Sew up side seam leaving bottom open.

FELTING

Put on rubber gloves.

Place apple in a basin with a small amount of cold water and a dash of detergent.

Make sure the fabric has soaked up the cold water.

Rub the fabric between your hands, agitating in a circular motion—you will see the felting process start.

Next, throw the fabric into the basin approx. 20–30 times; this helps shock the fibers and felt them together.

Run the fabric under the tap to remove the soapy liquid.

Once you are happy with this, pour a kettle of boiling water over the fabric and into the basin, taking care to avoid splashing yourself.

Swish the fabric around and again pick up (taking care as the fabric will be hot), squeeze out water, and agitate between your hands—repeat this last process.

MATERIALS

Rowan Creative Focus Worsted* (75% wool, 25% alpaca, approx. 220 yd/200 m per 3½ oz/100 g ball)

1 x shade 2055 Carmine

*If you wish to use a substitute yarn, make sure it is suitable for felting.

2-in (5-cm) square lime green felt fabric for leaf

2-in x 1-in (5-cm x 2-cm) strip brown felt fabric for stalk

Detergent

Thread to match leaf and stalk

Thread to match apple

Toy stuffing

EQUIPMENT

1 pair size US 7 (4.5 mm) knitting needles

Tapestry needle

Rubber gloves for felting

Basin

Long sharp sewing needle

GAUGE

Approx. 20 sts x 24 rows = 4 in (10 cm) in stockinette stitch (before felting)

TEMPLATE

See page 123

Once fabric is suitably felted, pour out the water, and rinse fabric in cold water.

Lay on a towel, fold the towel over, covering up the fabric, then roll up.

Squeeze the towel—to help remove excess water.

Remove fabric from towel—gently pull out into apple shape, then let dry.

MAKE LEAF/STALK

Cut leaf shape out of lime green felt fabric and leave to one side.

Next, using the template, cut out the stalk shape from brown felt fabric. Fold in half and sew down the open edge using backstitch or running stitch and leave to one side.

FINISHING

Once the apple has dried completely, insert stuffing from the bottom; make sure it is packed firmly. Once you are happy with the shape, sew up the bottom opening.

Next, create the indentation to give apple its shape. Using the long sharp needle and a long piece of matching thread, insert the needle from the bottom, up toward the top, and then back down to the bottom.

Tie the two loose ends together in a double knot, and pull tightly to make the indentation.

Next sew the leaf to the base of the stalk, then pin and stitch the stalk at the indentation.

golden pear

Who would have thought that the simple pear had so much mythology and symbolism behind it? It was sacred to Venus and Juno, as well as being the ancient Chinese symbol of immortality... Worked on two needles from bottom to top, the shape is created using basic increasing and decreasing techniques, and the change of color toward the top just adds to the look.

Using size US 7 (4.5 mm) needles and yarn A, cast on 11 sts.

Row 1 (WS): Purl to end.

Row 2: K1, *M1 by picking up the strand in between stitches and knitting into the back, K1, repeat from * to last st, K1 (20 sts).

Row 3: Purl to end.

Row 4: K1, *M1, K2, rep from * to last st, K1 (29 sts).

Row 5: Purl to end.

Row 6: K1, *M1, K3, rep from * to last st, K1 (38 sts).

Row 7: Purl to end.

Row 8: K1, *M1, K4, rep from * to last st, K1 (47 sts).

Starting with a purl row, work in stockinette stitch for 5 rows.

Row 14: K1, * K2tog, K3, rep from * to last st, K1 (38 sts).

Starting with a purl row, work in stockinette stitch for 3 rows.

Row 18: K1, * K2tog, K2, rep from * to last st, K1 (29 sts).

Break off yarn A and join in yarn B.

Starting with a purl row, work in stockinette stitch for 5 rows.

Row 24: K1, * K2tog, K1, rep from * to last st, K1 (20 sts).

Starting with a purl row, work in stockinette stitch for 3 rows.

Row 28: K1, * K2tog, rep from * to last st, K1 (11 sts).

Starting with a purl row, work in stockinette stitch for 5 rows.

Next row: K1, * K2tog, rep from * to last 2 sts, K2 (7 sts).

Break off yarn leaving a good length, thread through 7 sts on needle and pull tight, then secure.

Sew side seam leaving bottom open.

FELTING

Put on your rubber gloves.

Place pear in a basin with a small amount of cold water and a dash of detergent.

Make sure the fabric has soaked up the cold water.

Rub the fabric between your hands, agitating in a circular motion—you will see the felting process start.

Next, throw the fabric into the basin approx. 20–30 times, this helps shock the fibers and felt them together.

Run the fabric under the tap to remove the soapy liquid.

MATERIALS

Rowan Creative Focus Worsted (75% wool, 25% alpaca, approx. 220 yd/ 200 m per 3½ oz/100 g ball)
A shade 03810 Saffron
B shade 0018 Golden heather

If you wish to use a substitute yarn make sure it is suitable for felting.

2-in (5-cm) square lime green felt fabric for leaf

2-in x 1-in (5-cm x 2-cm) strip brown felt fabric for stalk

Detergent

Thread to match leaf and stalk

Toy stuffing

Thread to match pear

EQUIPMENT

1 pair size US 7 (4.5 mm) knitting needles

Tapestry needle

Long, sharp sewing needle

Rubber gloves for felting

Basin

GAUGE

Approx. 20 sts x 24 rows = 4 in (10 cm) in stockinette stitch (before felting)

TEMPLATE

See page 123

Once you are happy with the felting, pour a kettle of boiling water over the fabric and into the basin, taking care to avoid splashing yourself.

Swish the fabric around and again pick up (taking care as the fabric will be hot), squeeze out water, and agitate between your hands—repeat this last process.

Once fabric is suitably felted, pour out the water, and rinse fabric in cold water.

Lay on a towel, fold the towel over covering up the fabric, then roll up. Squeeze the towel to help remove excess water.

Remove fabric from towel, gently pull out into pear shape, then leave to dry.

LEAF/STALK

Cut leaf shape out of felt fabric and leave to one side.

Next, using the given template, cut out the stalk shape from brown felt fabric. Fold in half and sew down the open edge using back or running stitch and set aside.

FINISHING

Once the pear has dried completely, insert stuffing from the bottom; make sure it is packed firmly. Once you are happy with the shape, sew up the bottom opening.

Next sew the leaf to the base of the stalk, then pin and stitch the stalk to the top of the pear.

phone cover

This phone cover is a simple strip using a combination of knit and purl rows to create the folds, but what really makes it stand out is the bleached stencil spots. You can stencil any pattern onto the fabric—get your creative juices flowing!

Front and back are worked in
  1 piece.
Using size US 6 (4 mm) needles,
  cast on 15 sts.
Row 1: Knit to end.
Row 2: Purl to end.
Row 3: Knit to end.
Row 4: Repeat row 3.
Starting with a knit row, work
  37 rows in stockinette stitch.
Next row: Knit to end.
Starting with a knit row, work
  37 rows in stockinette stitch.
Next row: Knit to end.
Starting with a knit row, work
  3 rows in stockinette stitch.
Bind off.

BLEACHING

Wash knitted item as per
  instructions on ball band to fix
  the dye.
Leave fabric to dry.
Once dry, place fabric with right
  side facing on a few layers
  of newspaper, then place on
  ironing board, and pin out to
  correct shape. The newspaper
  will protect the ironing board
  surface.
Next place template on fabric.
Place a small amount of bleach
  in a saucer and, wearing rubber
  gloves, use the sponge to dab it
  onto the fabric to create
  the pattern.

Keep dabbing until you are
  happy with the shade the
  bleach has created.
Remove template and rinse
  fabric in hot soapy water to
  remove any excess bleach.
Let dry.
Once dry, use backstitch to
  embroider around the circular
  bleached-out shapes.

ASSEMBLY

Sew up the side seams working
  from the top down—weave in
  any loose ends.
Next fold the top over to create
  casing and stitch on the inside.
  Leave a small section open
  so you can insert the elastic
  through the casing you have
  just created.
Next thread the tapestry needle
  with the elastic, insert at the
  gap you have left, and run
  through.
Knot the ends of the elastic
  together—make sure you leave
  enough stretch so your phone
  will fit in.

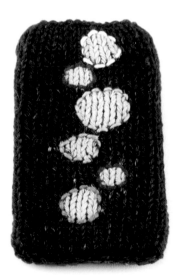

pencil case

Keep all your pencils and pens in place with this stripy zip-up pencil case. The case is knitted in a single strip with a bit of clever sewing up at the ends to create the flat-bottomed shape. The zipper is sewn into place before closing the ends, which makes it much easier to insert.

Using yarn A and size US 3 (3.25 mm) needles, cast on 35 sts.
Work 4 rows in garter stitch.
Change to yarn B.
Work 2 rows in stockinette stitch.
Change to yarn A and work 2 rows in stockinette stitch.
Last 4 rows form stripe pattern, keep working in 2-row stripe throughout.
Work 3 more rows in stockinette stitch ending on a knit row.
Next row (WS): Knit to end.
Work 11 more rows in stockinette stitch ending on a knit row.

Next row (WS): Knit to end.
Work 7 more rows in stockinette stitch keeping stripe pattern correct.
Next work 3 rows in garter stitch ending on a WS row.
Bind off knitwise.

ASSEMBLY

Weave in all loose ends, then block and press fabric to correct size.
Next pin and sew zipper into position along cast-on and bound-off edges.
Sew down side edges.

MATERIALS

Yarn: Rowan Handknit Cotton DK (100% cotton, approx. 93 yd/85 m per 1¾ oz/50g ball)

A shade 215 Rosso

B shade 219 Gooseberry

1 x 7¼-in (18-cm) zipper

EQUIPMENT

1 pair size US 3 (3.25 mm) knitting needles

Tapestry needle

Sharp sewing needle and thread to match fabric

GAUGE

Approx. 22 sts x 30 rows = 4 in (10 cm) in stockinette stitch

FINISHED SIZE

Approx. 6¼ in x 4 in (16 cm x 10 cm)

baby pixie hat

This elongated pixie hat idea is adapted from a basic beanie, simply by adding extra rows between the decreases to make the pointed shape. The hat is worked in a 2-row stripe throughout so there is no need to keep breaking off and joining in colors, and you will have hardly any ends to sew in. Simply insert the needle into the first stitch knitwise and bring up the color you want to work with.

MATERIALS

Rowan Creative Focus
Worsted (75% wool, 25%
alpaca, approx. 220 yd/200
m per 3½ oz/100 g ball)
A shade 01107 Cobalt
B shade 3089 Blue smoke

EQUIPMENT

1 pair size US 8 (5 mm)
knitting needles
1 pair size US 10 (6 mm)
knitting needles
Tapestry needle

GAUGE

Approx. 14 sts x 20 rows
= 4 in (10 cm) in stockinette
stitch with 2 strands of yarn
using size US 10 (6 mm)
knitting needles

FINISHED SIZE

To fit head circumference up
to 17 in (44 cm)

Use 2 strands of yarn held together throughout—take one end from the center of the ball and one end from the outside.

Using yarn A and size US 8 (5 mm) needles, cast on 43 sts.

Row 1: K1, * P1, K1, rep from * to end.

Row 2: P1, * K1, P1 rep from * to end.

Repeat last 2 rows once more.

Do not break off yarn A, join and start working with yarn B.

Change to size US 10 (6 mm) needles.

Starting with a knit row, work 6 rows in stockinette stitch.

Row 11: * K5, K2tog, rep from * to last st, K1 (37 sts).

Starting with a purl row, work 7 rows in stockinette stitch.

Row 19: * K4, K2tog, rep from * to last st, K1 (31 sts).

Starting with a purl row, work 5 rows in stockinette stitch.

Row 25: * K3, K2tog, rep from * to last st, K1 (25 sts).

Starting with a purl row, work 5 rows in stockinette stitch.

Row 31: * K2, K2tog, rep from * to last st, K1 (19 sts).

Starting with a purl row, work 3 rows in stockinette stitch.

Row 35: * K1, K2tog, rep from * to last st, K1 (13 sts).

Starting with a purl row, work 3 rows in stockinette stitch.

Row 39: K1, * K2tog, rep from * to last 2 sts, K2 (8 sts).

Next row: Purl to end.

Break off yarn leaving enough length to sew down side seam.

Using tapestry needle, slip sts from knitting needle onto yarn, pull tight, and secure.

Next sew the side seam from top toward cast-on edge using mattress stitch.

Weave in loose ends.

For finishing touch make a small pompom with yarn B and attach to top of hat.

◄ projects

strawberry beanie

This hat is worked from the top down, starting at the stalk and using increasing techniques, knitted in stockinette stitch toward the roll-edge brim. The seeds are stitched on once the hat has been completed using duplicate stitch, and the cute little leaf decoration is cut from felt fabric and stitched into position around the stalk.

Use 2 strands of yarn together throughout—take one end from the center of the ball and one end from the outside.

Using yarn B and size US 8 (5 mm) needles, cast on 6 sts.

Starting with a knit row, work 6 rows in stockinette stitch.

Break off yarn B and join yarn A.

Change to size US 10.5 (7 mm) needles.

Row 1: K1, (M1, K1) 4 times, K1 (10 sts).

Starting with a purl row, work 3 rows in stockinette stitch.

Row 5: K1, (M1, K1) 9 times, K1 (19 sts).

Row 6: Purl to end.

Row 7: K3, *M1, K3, rep from * to last st, M1, K1 (25 sts).

Row 8: Purl to end.

Row 9: K4, *M1, K4, rep from * to last st, M1, K1 (31 sts).

Starting with a purl row, work 3 rows in stockinette stitch.

Row 13: K5, *M1, K5, rep from * to last st, M1, K1 (37 sts).

Starting with a purl row, work 3 rows in stockinette stitch.

Row 17: K6, *M1, K6, rep from * to last st, M1, K1 (43 sts).

Starting with a purl row, work 10 rows in stockinette stitch.

Bind off knitwise.

ASSEMBLY

Sew up back seam using mattress stitch technique for stockinette stitch, working from the top down—remember to change to reverse stockinette stitch technique where the roll edge begins at the bound-off edge.

Using picture as guide work duplicate stitch technique with yellow yarn—using 2 strands together.

Work the stitches 3 rows apart and 3 stitches in between.

Cut the leaf shape out of green felt fabric using the template—snip a small hole at the center and slip over the stalk and down onto the hat.

Stitch into position.

MATERIALS

Rowan Pure Wool fisherman weight (100% wool, approx. 186 yd/170 m per 3½ oz/ 100 g ball)

A shade 679 Ember

Rowan Pure Wool worsted weight (100% wool, approx. 137 yd/125 m per 1¾ oz/ 50 g ball)

B shade 018 Earth

Approx. 4 in (10 cm) square lime green felt fabric for leaf

Small amount of yellow yarn for seeds

Thread to match felt

EQUIPMENT

1 pair size US 10.5 (7 mm) knitting needles

1 pair size US 8 (5 mm) knitting needles

Tapestry needle

Sewing needle

GAUGE

Approx 13 sts x 17.5 rows = 4 in (10 cm) in stockinette stitch with 2 ends of Aran weight yarn using size US 10.5 (7 mm) needles

FINISHED SIZE

13½ in (34 cm) circumference

TEMPLATE

See page 124

teddy bear baby hat

Make a simple beanie baby hat extra special with teddy bear ears. The hat is knitted using two strands of fisherman-weight yarn together throughout; basic decreasing techniques are used to create the rounded top. The ears are made separately and stitched into position at the top. You can easily use a different color for the ears to make them stand out even more.

MATERIALS

Rowan Creative Focus Worsted (75% wool, 25% alpaca, approx. 220 yd/ 200 m per 3½ oz/100 g ball) 1 x shade 018 Golden heather

EQUIPMENT

1 pair size US 8 (5 mm) knitting needles

1 pair size US 10 (6 mm) knitting needles

Tapestry needle

GAUGE

Approx. 14 sts x 20 rows = 4 in (10 cm) in stockinette stitch with 2 strands of yarn using size US 10 (6 mm) knitting needles

FINISHED SIZE

To fit head up to 17 in (44 cm) circumference

Use 2 strands of yarn together throughout—take one end from the center of the ball and one end from the outside.

Using size US 8 (5 mm) needles, cast on 43 sts.

Work 6 rows in garter stitch.

Change to size US 10 (6 mm) needles.

Starting with a knit row, work 4 rows in stockinette stitch.

Row 11: * K5, K2tog, rep from * to last st, K1 (37 sts).

Starting with a purl row, work 3 rows in stockinette stitch.

Row 15: * K4, K2tog, rep from * to last st, K1 (31 sts).

Starting with a purl row, work 3 rows in stockinette stitch.

Row 19: * K3, K2tog, rep from * to last st, K1 (25 sts).

Starting with a purl row, work 3 rows in stockinette stitch.

Row 23: * K2, K2tog, rep from * to last st, K1 (19 sts).

Row 24: Purl to end.

Row 25: * K1, K2tog, rep from * to last st, K1 (13 sts).

Row 26: P1 * P2tog, rep from * to end (7 sts).

Break off yarn leaving enough length to sew side seam.

Using tapestry needle, slip sts from knitting needle onto yarn, pull tight, and secure.

Next sew the side seam from top toward cast-on edge using mattress stitch.

Weave in loose ends.

EARS *make 2*

Using size US 10 (6 mm) needles and 2 strands of yarn held together as for hat, cast on 14 sts.

Work 2 rows of garter st.

Next row: K1, * K2tog, rep from * to last st, K1 (8 sts).

Break off yarn and slip sts on needle onto yarn—leave a long enough length to sew ear to hat.

Pull yarn tight to form a semicircle—secure yarn.

Next, using picture as guide, pin into position on hat and sew in place.

Repeat for second ear.

Weave in loose ends.

tiny kitty

This purrfectly formed little kitty is so cute—why not make a whole bunch of them? Add stripes and spots of embroidery to make your kitty even cuter.

BODY

Using size US 3 (3.25 mm) needles, cast on 7 sts.

Row 1: Purl to end.

Row 2: K1, *M1, K1, rep from * to last st, K1 (12 sts).

Starting with a purl row, work 7 rows in stockinette stitch.

Row 10: K1, * K2tog, rep from * to last st, K1 (7 sts).

Break off yarn—leaving a long enough length to sew seam.

Using tapestry needle, slip sts from knitting needle onto yarn and pull tight, then sew down seam using mattress stitch technique, leaving end open to add stuffing.

HEAD

Using size US 3 (3.25 mm) needles, cast on 7 sts.

Starting with a purl row, work 3 rows in stockinette stitch.

Row 4: K1, M1 by picking up the strand in between stitches and knitting into the back, K to last st, M1, K1 (9 sts).

Starting with a purl row, work 3 rows in stockinette stitch.

Row 8: K1, M1, knit to last st, M1, K1 (11 sts).

Row 9: Purl to end.

Row 10: Repeat row 8 (13 sts).

Row 11: Purl to end.

Row 12: K1, K2togtbl, K to 3 sts, K2tog, K1 (11 sts).

Row 13: Purl to end.

Row 14: Repeat row 12 (9 sts).

Starting with a purl row, work 3 rows in stockinette stitch.

Row 17: Repeat row 12 (7 sts).

Starting with a purl row, work 3 rows in stockinette stitch.

Bind off.

TAIL

With double-pointed needles, cast on 4 sts. Work I-cord for 8 rows.

Break off yarn and slip sts onto yarn. Pull tight and secure yarn with a few backstitches, then run length of yarn down through the center of the I-cord.

LEGS *make 4*

With double-pointed needles, cast on 4 sts. Work I-cord for 7 rows.

Break off yarn and slip sts onto yarn. Pull tight, and secure yarn with a few backstitches, then run length of yarn down through the center of the I-cord.

ASSEMBLY

Block and press head gently.

Next fold in half with WS together and sew side seams of head using mattress stitch.

Leave bottom open for inserting stuffing.

Next insert stuffing into body, then close up back by running

MATERIALS

Rowan Creative Focus Worsted (75% wool, 25% alpaca, approx. 220 yd/ 200 m per 3½ oz/100 g ball) 1 x shade 2190 Copper

Toy stuffing

18-gauge (1 mm thick) craft wire approx. 8 in (20 cm) long

Black yarn for embroidering face

EQUIPMENT

1 pair size US 3 (3.25 mm) knitting needles

1 pair size US 3 (3.25 mm) double-pointed knitting needles

Tapestry needle

Pliers

a length of yarn in and out of cast-on edge and pulling tight—work a few stitches to secure and weave in loose ends.

Next insert stuffing into head—use a pencil or knitting needle to make sure the stuffing goes into the ears.

Next pin and stitch head to front of body—use picture as guide.

Pin and stitch tail into position at the other end of the body.

Attach legs as follows.

Cut 2 lengths of wire approx. 4 in (10 cm) each with pliers.

Insert through body where you want the legs to be—make sure you have the same amount at each side, and then bend the wire to

make legs, repeat this process for back legs. Double back the ends of the wire into tight loops to prevent any sharp ends poking through.

Next slip the legs onto the wire, then using length of yarn left from cast-on, sew legs onto the body.

Embroider face, using illustration as a guide. Weave in any loose ends.

tiny teddy

Put all of your knitting skills together to create this tiny teddy. It's basically a knitted tube with a tiny bit of shaping to create the head. The arms are made from a rolled-up stockinette stitch tube inserted into position through the body. The legs are made from I-cords and stitched into position along the base of the body. And why not give your tiny ted his own personality with a pair of contrasting ears?

MATERIALS

Rowan Creative Focus Worsted (75% wool, 25% alpaca, approx. 22 yd/200 m per 3½ oz/100 g ball)
1 x shade 018 Golden heather

Toy stuffing

Black yarn for embroidering face

EQUIPMENT

1 pair size US 3 (3.25 mm) knitting needles

1 pair size US 3 (3.25 mm) double-pointed knitting needles

Tapestry needle

Pencil

Embroidery needle

BODY

Using size US 3 (3.25 mm) needles, cast on 16 sts.

Starting with a knit row, work in stockinette stitch for 14 rows.

Decrease for neck.

Row 15: K1, * K2tog, rep from * to last sts, K1 (9 sts).

Row 16: Purl to end.

Increase for head.

Row 17: K1,* KFB, rep from * to last st, K1 (16 sts).

Starting with a purl row, work 7 rows of stockinette stitch.

Next row: Repeat row 15 (9 sts).

Break off yarn leaving 8 in (20 cm).

Using tapestry needle, slip stitches from knitting needle onto yarn and pull tight and secure. Next, sew seam using mattress stitch—sew toward neck decrease, then insert stuffing into head.

Continue sewing seam toward cast-on edge and secure yarn by working a few stitches around the seam to the inside. Next insert stuffing into body.

Sew the front and back of the bottom seam together.

Set aside.

ARMS *make 1*

Using size US 3 (3.25 mm) needles, cast on 6 sts.

Starting with a knit row, work in stockinette stitch for 18 rows.

Bind off.

Allow the stockinette stitch to roll up on itself, and then sew down the long edge to secure.

LEGS *make 2*

Using size US 3 (3.25 mm) double-pointed needles, cast on 4 sts and work I-cord for approx. 7 rows.

Break off yarn and slip stitches onto the yarn—pull tight.

ASSEMBLY

Place arms as follows—using the point of a double-pointed needle, insert from right to left through the body where you want the arms to sit—wiggle the needle to make the hole slightly larger, then remove the needle.

Next take a sharp pencil and insert it back through the same hole to make it larger again. Twirl the pencil around to make a definite hole through the body.

Next insert arms as follows: Thread a spare piece of yarn through one end of the arm—thread both ends of the yarn through the tapestry needle. Next, insert the tapestry needle through the hole, and pull arm through so that both ends are even. Work a few stitches where the arms come out of the body to secure.

Sew the legs into position along the bottom seam of the body using the tail left after slipping the stitches off the needle.

Weave in any loose ends.

FINISHING

Make 2 ears as follows:

Using size US 3 (3.25 mm) needles, cast on 5 sts.

Work 2 rows of knit, then break off yarn leaving 8 in (10 cm), slip the stitches onto yarn, and pull tight, allowing the fabric to curl up and form ear shape.

Next, using length of yarn the stitches were slipped onto, sew the ears onto the head at the desired position.

Weave in all loose ends.

Next, using picture as guide, embroider face onto teddy.

Work 2 French knots for eyes and satin stitch for nose/mouth.

rib lace pompom hat

Keep cozy in style this winter with this quick and easy hat. Using a super bulky weight yarn and simple lace pattern you will have it knitted up in no time. The lace pattern is created by adding in and taking away stitches, and it's worked on the knit section of the rib, which really makes it stand out.

Using size US 17 (12 mm) needles, cast on 38 sts.

Row 1: P2, * K2, P2, rep from * to end.

Row 2: K2, * P2, K2, rep from * to end.

Row 3: P2, * K2tog, yo, P2, rep from * to end.

Row 4: Repeat row 2.

Row 5: Repeat row 1.

Row 6: Repeat row 2.

Row 7: P2, * keep yarn at front of work, K2togtbl, P2, rep from * to end.

Row 8: Repeat row 2.

The last 8 rows form rib lace pattern. Repeat rows 1–8 once more.

Row 17: Repeat row 1.

Row 18 (dec): K2, * P2tog, K2, rep from * to end (29 sts).

Row 19: P2, * K1, P2, rep from * to end.

Row 20: K2, * P1, K2, rep from * to end.

Repeat the last 2 rows twice more, then repeat row 19 once more.

Row 24: K2tog, * P1, K2tog, rep from * to end (20 sts).

Break off yarn—leaving a long enough length to sew back seam.

Using tapestry needle, slip sts from knitting needle onto yarn, pull tight, and secure.

ASSEMBLY

Do not block and press as this will flatten ribbed lace fabric.

Sew back seam using mattress stitch technique for reverse stockinette stitch.

FINISHING

Make large pompom as follows:

Wrap yarn approx 45 times around 6-in (15-cm) length of stiff cardboard or similar.

Next, keeping yarn around cardboard, tie separate pieces of spare yarn around top and then bottom of wrappings.

Next slip yarn off of cardboard—tie long length of yarn used around center of wrapping, making sure this is secure as it will form the center of the pompom.

Next, using sharp scissors, cut around pompom.

Give pompom a good shake to open out all the fibers and snip into shape. Do not cut the long ties that hold it together.

Thread tapestry needle with the longer lengths of yarn that you used to secure the pompom, thread down through the center top of hat, turn hat inside out, and secure.

MATERIALS

Rowan Big Wool (100% wool, approx. 88 yd/80 m per 3½ oz/100 g ball)
1 x shade 001 White hot
Cardboard

EQUIPMENT

1 pair size US 17 (12 mm) knitting needles
Tapestry needle
Scissors

GAUGE

Approx. 8 sts x 11 rows = 4 in (10 cm) in stockinette stitch

FINISHED SIZE

To fit average adult

ladybug key ring

Keep your keys together in style with this fab ladybug key ring. The design is made up from a simple knitted disk, and then decorated with felt fabric to create the distinctive ladybug pattern.

Using size US 3 (3.25 mm) needles, cast on 47 sts.

Row 1 (WS): Purl to end.

Row 2: K1, *K2tog, K3, rep from * to last st, K1 (38 sts).

Row 3: Purl to end.

Row 4: K1, *K2tog, K2, rep from * to last st, K1 (29 sts).

Row 5: Purl to end.

Row 6: K1, *K2tog, K1, rep from * to last st, K1 (20 sts).

Row 7: Purl to end.

Row 8: K1, *K2tog, rep from * to last st, K1 (11 sts).

Break off yarn leaving 16 in (40 cm), thread through 11 sts on needle and pull tight, then secure. Sew side seam to form a disk.

Using size US 3 (3.25 mm) needles, pick up 3 sts along top edge—opposite side from seam.

Starting with a purl row, work in stockinette stitch for approx. 12 rows or until required length is reached.

Slip key ring onto strip, fold in half, and sew strip into a loop.

ASSEMBLY

Weave in loose ends, then block and press.

FINISHING

Using templates, cut out the head, spots, and center spike from black felt. Using picture as guide, sew the felt pieces into place.

Next cut backing out of gray felt fabric, and then sew into position on the underside of ladybug.

MATERIALS

Yarn: Rowan Cotton Glace (100% cotton, approx. 127 yd/116 m per 1¾ oz/50g ball) 1 x shade 741 Poppy

1 double-loop metal key ring

Approx. 4 in (10 cm) square black felt fabric

Black thread

Approx. 4 in (10 cm) square gray felt fabric for backing

EQUIPMENT

1 pair size US 3 (3.25 mm) knitting needles

Tapestry needle

Sharp sewing up needle

GAUGE

Approx. 25 sts x 32 rows = 4 in (10 cm) in stockinette stitch

TEMPLATE

See page 124

bumblebee key ring

If you are a busy bee and need to keep your keys in place, this bumblebee key ring is for you. The simple knitted disk is decorated with felt fabric go-faster stripes, and sweet little wings give this project its must-have appeal.

Using size US 3 (3.25 mm) needles, cast on 47 sts.

Row 1 (WS): Purl to end.

Row 2: K1, * K2tog, K3, rep from * to last st, K1 (38 sts).

Row 3: Purl to end.

Row 4: K1, * K2tog, K2, rep from * to last st, K1 (29 sts).

Row 5: Purl to end.

Row 6: K1, * K2tog, K1, rep from * to last st, K1 (20 sts).

Row 7: Purl to end.

Row 8: K1, * K2tog, rep from * to last st, K1 (11 sts).

Break off yarn leaving 16 in (40 cm), thread through 11 sts on needle and pull tight, then secure. Sew up side seam to form a disk.

ASSEMBLY

Weave in loose ends, then block and press.

FINISHING

Slip key belt clip onto the nylon strapping. Fold the strapping in half and place at the top center of the knitted disk; sew into position using black thread.

Using templates, cut out the stripes from yellow felt fabric, and then the bottom, sting, and wings from white. Using picture as guide, sew the felt pieces into place.

Place eyes as follows: Thread sharp sewing needle with black thread, and then place sequin into position on head. Bring the needle up through the knitted fabric and out through the middle of the sequin, then place the bead onto the needle and slip down so it sits on the sequin. Bring the needle back down through the sequin and fabric. Work a couple of backstitches with the thread to secure.

Next cut backing out of gray felt fabric, and then sew into position on the underside of bumblebee.

MATERIALS

Rowan Cotton Glace (100% cotton, approx. 127 yd/116 m per 1¾ oz/50 g ball)
1 x shade 727 Black

Approx. 6-in (15-cm) square black felt fabric

Approx. 4-in (10-cm) square yellow felt fabric

Approx. 6-in (15-cm) square white felt fabric

Approx. 4-in (10-cm) square gray felt fabric for backing

2 black beads for eyes

2 white sequins for eyes

Black thread

1 metal belt key clip

Approx. 2½ in (6 cm) nylon strapping

EQUIPMENT

1 pair size US 3 (3.25 mm) knitting needles

Tapestry needle

Sharp sewing up needle

GAUGE

Approx. 25 sts x 32 rows – 4 in (10 cm) in stockinette stitch

TEMPLATE

See page 124

ear warmer

The ear warmer has really grown in popularity in recent winters. This one is worked in one continuous length and, by increasing and decreasing, the band is made slightly broader toward the front. The cable twist adds a bit of interest and texture to the fabric.

Using size US 15 (10 mm) needles, cast on 8 sts.
Row 1: Knit to end.
Row 2: K2, P4, K2.
Repeat last 2 rows twice more.
Row 7: K2, CF4, K2.
Row 8: Repeat row 2.
Row 9: Repeat row 1.
Row 10: Repeat row 2.
Row 11: K2, M1 by picking up the strand in between the stitches and knitting into the back, K4, M1, K2 (10 sts).
Row 12: K2, P6, K2.
Row 13: Knit to end.
Row 14: Repeat row 12.
Row 15: K2, CF6, K2.
Row 16: Repeat row 12.
Row 17: Repeat row 13.
Repeat the last 2 rows once more, then next row as row 12 again.
Row 21: K2, M1, K6, M1, K2 (12 sts).
Row 22: K2, P8, K2.
Row 23: K2, CF8, K2.
Row 24: Repeat row 22.
Row 25: Knit to end.
Repeat last 2 rows twice more, then row 24 once more.
Row 31: Repeat row 23.
Work the next 2 rows as rows 24 and 25, then row 24 once more.
Row 35: K2, K2togtbl, K4, K2tog, K2 (10 sts).

Row 36: Repeat row 12.
Row 37: Knit to end.
Row 38: Repeat row 12.
Row 39: Repeat row 15.
Work the next 5 rows as rows 16–20.
Row 45: K2, K2togtbl, K2, K2tog, K2 (8 sts).
Row 46: Repeat row 2.
Row 47: Repeat row 7.
Row 48: Repeat row 2.
Row 49: Knit to end.
Repeat the last 2 rows twice more, then row 2 once more.
Bind off.
Break off yarn leaving enough length to sew narrow ends together.

FINISHING
Do not block and press as this will flatten the cable twist.
Bring the narrow ends together to form a ring, then sew ends together.

MATERIALS

Yarn: Rowan Big Wool (100% wool, approx. 88 yd/80 m per 3½ oz/ 100 g ball)
A shade 054 Vert

EQUIPMENT

1 pair size US 15 (10 mm) knitting needles
Cable needle
Tapestry needle

GAUGE

Approx. 9½ sts x 12 rows = 4 in (10 cm) in stockinette stitch

FINISHED SIZE

To fit average adult

arm warmers

Keep your arms nice and cozy with these ribbed arm warmers. Knitted using a super bulky yarn in a 2 x 1 reverse rib pattern, the arm warmers are finished off with a contrast block stripe to the top, but you can create your own stripe pattern to make this design your own. For a smaller size, simply cast on fewer stitches.

ARM WARMER *make 2*

Using size US 15 (10 mm) needles and yarn A, cast on 20 sts.

Row 1: P2, *K1, P2 rep from * to end.

Row 2: K2, * P1, K2, rep from * to end.

The last 2 rows form rib pattern, repeat until 22 rows have been worked.

Break off yarn A and join yarn B.

Work 5 rows in rib pattern, ending with a RS row.

Bind off in knit.

FINISHING

Weave in all loose ends—do not block and press as this will flatten the rib pattern.

With right side facing sew up using mattress stitch for reverse stockinette stitch.

Weave in loose ends.

MATERIALS

Rowan Big Wool (100% wool, approx. 88 yd/80 m per 3½ oz/100 g ball)
A shade 063 Lipstick
B shade 026 Blue velvet

EQUIPMENT

1 pair size US 15 (10 mm) knitting needles

Tapestry needle

GAUGE

Approx. 9 sts x 12 rows = 4 in (10 cm) in stockinette stitch

FINISHED SIZE

To fit average adult. For smaller sizes cast on 14 sts/ 17 sts and work pattern as is.

bracelet

Why not give an old accessory a new lease of life? Revamp an existing bracelet or customize a new one with this multistripe knitted band. Go crazy with the colors—it's a great way to use up all the scraps of yarn left over from other projects. You can weave in the ends as you go to reduce the amount of finishing.

Using size US 3 (3.25 mm) needles and yarn D, cast on 15 sts.

Starting with a knit row work in stockinette stitch throughout.

Rows 1–4: D, red.
Row 5: I, yellow.
Rows 6–7: G, pink.
Rows 8–10: B, turquoise.
Rows 11–12: H, black.
Row 13: D, red.
Rows 14–15: A, blue.
Rows 16–17: E, ecru.
Rows 18–19: B, turquoise.
Rows 20–21: F, lilac.
Rows 22–23: A, blue.
Rows 24–29: C, green.
Row 30: D, red.
Rows 31–33: G, pink.
Rows 34–35: D, red.
Row 36: I, yellow.
Row 37: H, black.
Rows 38–40: A, blue.
Row 41: D, red.
Rows 42–43: E, ecru.
Row 44: G, pink.
Rows 45–46: B, turquoise.
Rows 47–48: I, yellow.

Rows 49–51: A, blue.
Row 52: B, turquoise.
Row 53–54: A, blue.
Rows 55–57: D, red.
Rows 58–59: B, turquoise.
Row 60: H, black.
Rows 61–62: C, green.
Rows 63–66: G, pink.
Rows 67–68: A, blue.
Bind off.

FINISHING

Sew the bound-off edges together to make a ring, then slip the bracelet into the knitting with the right side of the stripes facing. Next wrap the fabric around the bracelet using safety pins to hold the seam together.

Using mattress stitch, sew along the straight edges, matching up the stripes as you go.

fingerless gloves

The basic 2 x 2 rib pattern is great for this type of project—it gives the fabric a slight stretch so that it sits snugly around your wrist and hand. Because the gloves are fingerless they are perfect for keeping your hands cozy but your fingers free.

MATERIALS

Rowan Renew (93% recycled wool, 7% polyamide, approx. 82 yd/75 m per 1¾ oz/ 50 g ball)
1 x shade 684 Garage

EQUIPMENT

1 pair size US 10 (6 mm) knitting needles
Tapestry needle

GAUGE

Approx. 14 sts x 20 rows = 4 in (10 cm) in stockinette stitch

FINISHED SIZE

To fit average adult

LEFT-HAND GLOVE

Using size US 10 (6 mm) needles, cast on 26 sts.
Row 1: K2, * P2, K2, rep from * to end.
Row 2: P2, * K2, P2, rep from * to end.
The last 2 rows form rib pattern. Repeat rows 1–2 5 more times.

PLACE THUMB

Row 13: K2, (P2, K2) twice, P1, M1 by picking up the strand in between the stitches and working into the back, P1, (K2, P2) 3 times, K2 (27 sts).
Row 14: (P2, K2) 3 times, P2, K3, P2, (K2, P2) twice.
Row 15: K2, (P2, K2) twice, P1, M1, P1, M1, P1, (K2, P2) 3 times, K2 (29 sts).
Row 16: (P2, K2) 3 times, P2, K5, P2, (K2, P2) twice.
Row 17: K2, (P2, K2) twice, P1, M1, P3, M1, P1, (K2, P2) 3 times, K2 (31 sts).
Row 18: (P2, K2) 3 times, P2, K7, P2, (K2, P2) twice.
Row 19: K2, (P2, K2) twice, P1, M1, P5, M1, P1, (K2, P2) 3 times, K2 (33 sts).
Row 20: (P2, K2) 3 times, P2, K9, P2, (K2, P2) twice.
Row 21: K2, (P2, K2) twice, P1, M1, P7, M1, P1, (K2, P2) 3 times, K2 (35 sts).
Row 22: (P2, K2) 3 times, P2,

K11, P2, (K2, P2) twice.
Next row: K2 (P2, K2) twice, P10, turn.
Next row: K9—these are the stitches that create the thumb—work on these 9 sts only.
Next row: P9.
Next row: K9.
Next row: P9.
Bind off 9 sts—break off yarn leaving enough length of yarn to sew thumb.
Sew thumb using mattress stitch technique for reverse stockinette stitch.
Next with RS facing using RH needle, rejoin yarn by picking up 2 sts at base of thumb—keeping rib sequence correct work to end of row (28 sts).
Next row: Rib 14 sts, K4, rib to end.
Next row: Rib 10 sts, P2togtbl, P2tog, rib to end (26 sts).
Work 10 more rows in rib pattern as set.
Bind off in rib.

RIGHT-HAND GLOVE

Work as given for left-hand glove until placing thumb.
Place thumb as follows:
Row 13: K2, (P2, K2) 3 times, P1, M1 by picking up the strand in between the stitches and working into the back, P1, (K2,

P2) twice, K2 (27 sts).

Row 14: (P2, K2) twice, P2, K3, P2, (K2, P2) 3 times.

Row 15: K2, (P2, K2) 3 times, P1, M1, P1, M1, P1, (K2, P2) twice, K2 (29 sts).

Row 16: (P2, K2) twice, P2, K5, P2, (K2, P2) 3 times.

Row 17: K2, (P2, K2) 3 times, P1, M1, P3, M1, P1, (K2, P2) twice, K2 (31 sts).

Row 18: (P2, K2) twice, P2, K7, P2, (K2, P2) 3 times.

Row 19: K2, (P2, K2) 3 times, P1, M1, P5, M1, P1, (K2, P2) twice, K2 (33 sts).

Row 20: (P2, K2) twice, P2, K9, P2, (K2, P2) 3 times.

Row 21: K2, (P2, K2) 3 times, P1, M1, P7, M1, P1, (K2, P2) twice, K2 (35 sts).

Row 22: (P2, K2) twice, P2, K11, P2, (K2, P2) 3 times.

Next row: K2 (P2, K2) 3 times, P10, turn.

Next row: K9—these are the stitches that create the thumb—work on these 9 sts only.

Next row: P9.

Next row: K9.

Next row: P9.

Bind off 9 sts—break off yarn leaving enough length of yarn to sew thumb.

Sew thumb using mattress stitch technique for reverse stockinette stitch.

Next with RS facing using RH needle, rejoin yarn by picking up 2 sts at base of thumb—keeping rib sequence correct work to end of row (28 sts).

Next row: Rib 10 sts, K4, rib to end.

Next row: Rib 14 sts, P2togtbl, P2tog, rib to end (26 sts).

Work 10 more rows in rib pattern as set.

Bind off in rib.

ASSEMBLY

Weave in loose ends—do not block and press as this will flatten the rib fabric.

Using spare length of yarn sew side seam using mattress stitch technique.

button-front neck warmer

This project is the perfect alternative to a scarf; the garter-stitch fabric sits snugly around your neck keeping you cozy on chilly days. Knitted in a super-bulky 100 percent merino wool for extra warmth, it's sure to become a winter wardrobe favorite.

Using size US 15 (10 mm) needles, cast on 16 sts.

Work in garter stitch for 56 rows.

Place buttonholes.

Row 57: K3, * yo, K2togtbl, K2, rep from * twice more, K1.

Work in garter stitch for 3 more rows.

Bind off knitwise.

Weave in ends.

Block and press gently if required to finished size.

Sew on buttons to match up with buttonholes.

MATERIALS

Rowan Drift (100% merino wool, approx. 87 yd/80 m per 3½ oz/100 g ball) 1 x shade 908 Shore

3 x 1¼-in (3-cm) buttons

EQUIPMENT

1 pair size US 15 (10 mm) knitting needles

Tapestry needle

GAUGE

8.5 sts x 15 rows = 4 in (10 cm) in garter stitch using size US 15 (10 mm) needles

FINISHED SIZE

Approx. 7 in x 23 in (18 cm x 58 cm)

1

2

3

4

lampshade decoration

This design is great for giving your decor a quick refresh—revamp an existing lampshade with this beaded braid design. The number of beads and the length you knit will depend on the size of the lampshade. A 30-minute knit will give you roughly 24 in (60 cm) once blocked and pressed, though the length may differ depending on your gauge.

Thread approx. 120 beads onto the yarn (see page 118). as follows:

Tip—it's better to have too many than not enough beads if you are unsure of the length you want to knit; you will use approx. 2 beads per ½ in (1 cm).

Using yarn A and size US 3 (3.25 mm) needles, cast on 5 sts.

Row 1: Knit to end.

Row 2: K1, P3, K1.

Row 3: K1, bead 1 (B1) as follows: Bring bead up to back of knitting, bring yarn forward to the front of work between needle, make sure bead is sitting at the front of work, slip the next stitch purlwise, then bring the yarn between the needles to the back of the work, wrapping the slipped stitch and making sure the bead is sitting to the front, K1, B1 as described, K1.

Row 4: Repeat row 2.
The last 4 rows form the pattern, repeat until required length.
Bind off.

ASSEMBLY

Weave in loose ends; make sure all the beads are sitting to the front.
Block and press to flatten strip.

MATERIALS

Rowan Cotton Glace (100% cotton, approx. 127 yd/116 m per 1¾ oz/50 g ball)

A shade 841 Garnet

B shade 844 Green slate

Debbie Abrahams beads, size US 8 (approx. 500 beads per packet)
A color 46
B color 36

EQUIPMENT

1 pair size US 3 (3.25 mm) knitting needles

Sharp sewing needle with 4-in (10-cm) loop of sewing thread to thread beads onto yarn

◂ projects

wrist corsage

Dress up your outfit with this floral wrist corsage. Each petal is worked individually then stitched together to form the flower shape. Add a dash of sparkle to the center with contrasting glass beads.

PETALS *make 5*

Using size US 3 (3.25 mm) needles, cast on 3 sts.

Row 1 (WS): Purl to end.

Row 2: K1, M1, K1, M1, K1 (5 sts).

Row 3: K1, P3, K1.

Row 4: K1, M1, K3, M1, K1 (7 sts).

Row 5: K1, P5, K1.

Row 6: K1, M1, K5, M1, K1 (9 sts).

Row 7: K1, P7, K1.

Row 8: Knit.

Row 9: Repeat row 7.

Row 10: K3, Sl2 knitwise, K1, psso, K3 (7 sts).

Row 11: Repeat row 5.

Row 12: K2, Sl2 knitwise, K1, psso, K2 (5 sts).

Row 13: Repeat row 3.

Row 14: K1, Sl2 knitwise, K1, psso, K1 (3 sts).

Row 15: P3tog.

ASSEMBLY

Weave in all loose ends, block, and press each petal.

Using picture as guide, sew petals together as follows: Using backstitch work from the center point of the petal up toward the outer edge for approx. 1 in (2 cm).

Using red thread, sew the beads into position at the center of the flower.

Next run the cord elastic through the back of the flower, then knot ends together to form a loop—make sure it will fit onto your wrist and sit snugly but not too tightly.

MATERIALS

Rowan Cotton Glace (100% cotton, approx. 127 yd/116 m per 1¾ oz/50 g ball)

1 x shade 741 Poppy

Red thread

Selection of beads for center decoration

Approx. 6 in (15 cm) cord elastic

EQUIPMENT

1 pair size US 3 (3.25 mm) knitting needles

Tapestry needle

GAUGE

Approx. 25 sts x 32 rows = 4 in (10 cm) in stockinette stitch

scented heart

This design is perfect for hanging on a door handle or over a coat hanger. The heart shape is created using shaping techniques then decorated on the front with cutout felt motifs and contrasting stitching. Use the scent of your choice; dried lavender or rosebuds are perfect.

HEART PANEL *make 2*

Using size US 3 (3.25 mm) needles, cast on 3 sts.

Row 1 (WS): Purl to end.

Row 2: (RS): K1, M1 by picking up loop in between sts and knitting into the back, K1, M1, K1 (5 sts).

Row 3: P1, M1 by picking up loop in between sts and working into the back, K3, M1, K1 (7 sts).

Row 4: K1, M1, knit to last st, M1, K1 (9 sts).

Row 5: Purl to end.

Row 6: Repeat row 4 (11 sts).

Row 7: Repeat row 5.

Row 8: Repeat row 4 (13 sts).

Starting with a purl row, work 3 rows in stockinette stitch.

Row 12: Repeat row 4 (15 sts).

Row 13: Repeat row 5.

Repeat the last 2 rows twice more (19 sts).

Row 18: Repeat row 4 (21 sts).

Starting with a purl row, work 5 rows in stockinette stitch.

Shape top as follows:

Next row: K1, K2togtbl, K7, turn—knit on these 9 sts only.

**Next row: P1, P2tog, purl to last 3 sts, P2togtbl, P1 (7 sts).

Next row: K1, K2togtbl, K1, K2tog, K1 (5 sts).

Next row: P1, P3tog, P1 (3 sts).

Bind off.

Rejoin yarn to remaining 11 sts.

Next row: Bind off 1, knit to last 3 sts, K2tog, K1 (9 sts).

Complete the pattern by working from ** on shaped top just worked.

ASSEMBLY

Weave in loose ends, then block and press to the correct size and shape.

Cut out the heart motifs from felt fabric using templates.

Layer the felt hearts and sew together, then place the motifs onto the front heart panel and stitch together.

Next, using red yarn, work a row of backstitch just in from the outer edge of the front panel—use picture as guide.

Next fold the velvet ribbon in half and stitch to the wrong side at the center of the back panel.

Next sew the front and back panels together, working from the point up toward the top—leave the top open and insert the scented filling.

Sew the top section of the heart.

picture frames

These mini passport-size picture frames are great for finishing off and adding that special something to your snaps. Working through the pattern will show you how a straightforward increasing technique can change a simple strip into a rectangle. Choose your favorite colors or add a simple stripe.

Using size US 3 (3.25 mm) needles, cast on 40 sts.

Row 1: Knit to end.

Row 2: K4, yo, K1, yo, K10, yo, K1, yo, K8, yo, K1, yo, K10, yo, K1, yo, K4 (48 sts).

Row 3: K4, ktbl, K1, ktbl, K10, ktbl, K1, ktbl, K8, ktbl, K1, ktbl, K10, ktbl, K1, ktbl, K4.

Row 4: K5, yo, K1, yo, K12, yo, K1, yo, K10, yo, K1, yo, K12, yo, K1, yo, K5 (56 sts).

Row 5: K5, ktbl, K1, ktbl, K12, ktbl, K1, ktbl, K10, ktbl, K1, ktbl, K12, ktbl, K1, ktbl, K5.

Row 6: K6, yo, K1, yo, K14, yo, K1, yo, K12, yo, K1, yo, K14, yo, K1, yo, K6 (64 sts).

Row 7: K6, ktbl, K1, ktbl, K14, ktbl, K1, ktbl, K12, ktbl, K1, ktbl, K14, ktbl, K1, ktbl, K6.

Bind off knitwise.

ASSEMBLY

Pin out to required size, then block and press.

Sew ends together to form frame, then weave in all loose ends.

MATERIALS

Rowan Cotton Glace (100% cotton, approx. 127 yd/116 m per 1¾ oz/50 g ball)
A shade 814 Shoot
B shade 812 Ivy
C shade 741 Poppy

EQUIPMENT

1 pair size US 3 (3.25 mm) knitting needles

Tapestry needle

GAUGE

Approx. 25 sts x 32 rows = 4 in (10 cm) in stockinette stitch

FINISHED SIZE

Approx. 1¾ in x 2 in (4 cm x 5 cm)

finger puppets

These fun finger puppets are all worked from the same basic pattern—but the "lady" puppet has the addition of a frilly skirt. The different characters are created by using different colors and a touch of embroidery. These puppets are brilliant for using up any scraps of yarn you have left over from other projects.

rabbit

BODY AND HEAD

Using size US 3 (3.25 mm) needles, cast on 16 sts.
Starting with a knit row work in stockinette stitch for 18 rows.
Shape top of head.
Row 15: K1, * K2tog, K1 rep from * to end (11 sts).
Row 16: Purl to end.
Next row: K1, *(K2tog) twice, K1, rep from * once more (7 sts).
Next row: Purl to end.
Break off yarn, slip sts on needle onto yarn, pull tight to gather the stitches together. Next sew toward the cast-on edge using mattress stitch technique. Secure yarn and weave in all loose ends.

EARS *make 2*

Using size US 3 (3.25 mm) needles, cast on 3 sts.
Work 2 rows in garter stitch.
Next row: K1, M1 by picking up the strand of yarn in between the stitches and knitting into the back, K1, M1, K1 (5 sts).
Work 12 more rows in garter stitch.
Next row: K1, Sl2 knitwise, K1, psso, K1 (3 sts).
Next row: Knit.
Break off yarn and pull through stitches on needle.

FINISHING

Using picture as guide sew ears into position on top of head— use the end of yarn that you slipped the stitches onto for sewing.
Weave in loose ends at top of ears.
Using picture as guide, work 2 French knots for eyes in black, then work nose using a satin stitch in pink and a backstitch for mouth. The tail is worked in a satin stitch using ecru or white.

projects

MATERIALS

Rabbit
Rowan Cotton Glace (100% cotton, approx. 127 yd/116 m per 1¾ oz/50 g ball)
1 x shade 843 Toffee

Small amount of pink and black yarns for face, and ecru/white for tail

Lady
Rowan Cotton Glace (100% cotton, approx. 127 yd/116 m per 1¾ oz/50 g ball)
For dress:
A shade 841 Garnet
B shade 832 Persimmon
For body:
C shade 725 Ecru
For hair:
Rowan Panama (55% viscose, 33% cotton, 12% linen, approx. 148 yd/135 m per 1¾ oz/50 g ball)
D shade 304 Orchid

Small amount of blue and red yarns for face

Pirate
Rowan Cotton Glace (100% cotton, approx. 127 yd/116 m per 1¾ oz/50 g ball)
A shade 850 Cobalt
B shade 727 Black
C shade 741 Poppy
D shade 726 Bleached
E shade 845 Shell

EQUIPMENT

1 pair size US 3 (3.25 mm) double-pointed needles

Tapestry needle

GAUGE

Approx. 25 sts x 32 rows = 4 in (10 cm) in stockinette stitch

lady

SKIRT

Using size US 3 (3.25 mm) needles and yarn A, cast on 32 sts.

Starting with a knit row, work 5 rows in stockinette stitch.

Row 6: * K2tog, rep from * to end (16 sts).

Slip onto spare needle—do not break off yarn.

BODY

Using size US 3 (3.25 mm) needles and yarn C, cast on 16 sts.

Starting with a knit row, work in stockinette stitch for 10 rows.

Attach skirt as follows:

Bring the spare needle with skirt stitches up to the needle with body stitches and hold parallel with both right sides facing you.

Then using yarn A, knit both sets together by inserting the needle into the first sts of both sets at the same time; work as you would normally for a knit stitch, and slip both stitches off, repeat to end.

Break off yarn A and join yarn B.

Work 3 rows in garter stitch.

Break off yarn B and join yarn A.

Starting with a knit row, work in stockinette stitch for 2 more rows, then purl 1 row.

Break off yarn A and join yarn C.

Starting with a knit row, work in stockinette stitch for 6 rows.

Shape top of head.

Next row: K1, * K2tog, K1, rep from * to end (11 sts).

Next row: Purl to end.

Next row: K1, *(K2tog) twice, K1, rep from * once more.

Next row: Purl to end.

Break off yarn, slip sts on needle onto yarn, pull tight to gather the stitches together, then sew toward

the cast-on edge using mattress stitch technique. Secure yarn and weave in all loose ends. Sew back seam of skirt.

ARMS *make 2*

With yarn C, cast on 4 sts and work I-cord for 7 rows.

Break off yarn and slip sts onto yarn, pull tight, and secure yarn with a few backstitches.

Attach to body just above where dress stops using end of yarn. Run unused length of yarn down through the center of I-cord.

FINISHING

Using picture as guide, embroider face onto front of head using duplicate stitch for eyes in blue and lips in red.

Cut approx. 16 lengths of yellow yarn and group together in sets of 2.

Fold in half and loop through the top of the head around the last row of stitches.

pirate

Work as given for rabbit in stripe sequence for 15 rows.

Rows 1–8: Blue.

Rows 9–10: Black.

Row 11: Red.

Row 12: White.

Repeat last 2 rows once more, then row 11 once more.

Change to pink yarn.

Starting with a knit row, work in stockinette stitch for 4 rows.

Shape top of head.

Next row: K1, * K2tog, K1, rep from * to end (11 sts).

Next row: Purl to end.

Break off pink and join red.

Next row: K1, *(K2tog) twice, K1, rep from * once more.

Next row: Purl to end.

Break off yarn, slip sts on needle onto yarn, pull tight to gather the stitches together, then sew toward the cast-on edge using mattress stitch technique. Secure yarn and weave in all loose ends.

Make arms as given for lady in pink.
Attach to body at base of head.
Using picture as guide, embroider face onto front of head using satin stitch for patch and French knot for eye in black. Then embroider belt buckle with gold or yellow yarn using backstitch.
Tie a small amount of yarn as a knot to the left-hand side of red yarn at top of the head.

coin purse

This drawstring coin purse with button stopper is small enough to fit in your pocket and perfect for keeping your loose change in one place. It can be knitted up in no time in a mix of simple stitches—a blank canvas for you to embellish and make your own.

Using size US 3 (3.25 mm) needles, cast on 17 sts.
Work 4 rows in garter stitch.
Place eyelets.
Row 5 (RS): K2,* K2togtbl, yo, K3, rep from * twice more, K2togtbl, yo, K1.
Starting with a purl row, work 20 more rows in stockinette stitch.
Next row (WS): Knit to end.
Starting with a knit row, work 20 more rows in stockinette stitch.
Place eyelets.
Next row (RS): K2,* K2togtbl, yo, K3, rep from * twice more, K2togtbl, yo, K1.
Work 4 rows in garter stitch.
Bind off knitwise.
Break off yarn and weave in loose ends.

ASSEMBLY
Block and press fabric so edges are flat. Do not press the garter stitch top and bottom.
Using mattress stitch, sew both side seams.
Using picture as guide, embroider flower motifs if desired.

DRAWSTRING
Using approx. 24 in (60 cm) of yarn, make twisted cord (see page 119).
Starting from the inside of the purse—making sure the knot is to the inside—thread the twisted cord in and out of the eyelets toward the other side seam, then thread cord in and out of button—only use 2 holes if you are using a 4-hole button. Then repeat the process, threading twisted cord in and out of eyelets back to the beginning. Knot the ends of the cord together.

MATERIALS
Rowan Pure Life Organic Cotton DK, naturally dyed (100% cotton, approx. 131 yd/120 m per 1¾ oz/50 g ball)
1 x shade 986 Natural

Odds and ends of scrap yarn for embroidery detail

1 x ¾-in (2-cm) button with 2 or 4 holes

EQUIPMENT
1 pair size US 3 (3.25 mm) knitting needles
Tapestry needle

GAUGE
Approx. 25 sts x 32 rows = 4 in (10 cm) in stockinette stitch

Salvador Dalí mustache

Whimsical and fun, this Dalí-inspired mustache is sure to brighten up your day. It is so simple to make; the mustache shape is created by knitting an I-cord (tube), and with the addition of bendy wire you can curl up the ends in any way you like.

With size US 3 (3.25 mm) needles, cast on 4 sts and work approx 30 rows of I-cord as follows.

Knit to the end of the row—do not turn, slide the stitches back up to the right-hand point of the needle, insert needle in right hand into the 1st stitch, bring the yarn from the left-hand side, and knit to the end of the row.

Repeat this process until 30 rows have been completed.

Now work back and forth on 2 needles.

Row 31: Purl to end.

Work 6 more rows in stockinette stitch.

Next row: K1, M1 by picking up the strand in between the 2 sts and knitting into the back, knit to end (5 sts).

Next row: K1, P3, K1.

Next row: Knit to end.

Next row: K1, P3, K1.

Next row: K1, K2togtbl, knit to end (4 sts).

Next work 8 more rows as I-cord, turn as if to work purl row.

Next row: K1, P2, K1.

Next row: K1, M1, knit to end (5 sts).

Next row: K1, P3, K1.

Next row: Knit to end.

Next row: K1, P3, K1.

Next row: K1, K2togtbl, knit to end (4 sts).

Next work 29 more rows as I-cord.

Bind off.

ASSEMBLY

Weave in loose ends, then gently press the flat pieces of knitting—do not press the I-cord section.

INSERT WIRE

Cut the wire with pliers to the same length as the knitting.

With the wrong side of mustache facing, insert the wire from right to left down through the center of all the I-cords.

Close the ends of the I-cords to keep the wire from coming out.

Next, using tapestry needle and same yarn as you have knitted with, stitch the wire to the top edge of the flat pieces of knitting.

Next, using picture as guide, curl up the edges of the mustache.

MATERIALS

Rowan Handknit Cotton (100% cotton, approx. 93 yd/85 m per 1¾ oz/50 g ball)
1 x shade 252 Black

1.2 mm silver wire, approx. 20 in (50 cm)

EQUIPMENT

1 pair size US 3 (3.25 mm) double-pointed needles

Pliers

Tapestry needle

bow hairpins

This cute yet simple accessory is an essential whatever the length of your hair. Add a sprinkling of beads if you fancy a bit of sparkle. It's worked in a sportweight yarn and the bow shape is created using straightforward increasing and decreasing techniques. The pin is secured to the back of the bow and the strip of contrasting felt fabric finishes off the project perfectly.

PLAIN BOW

With size US 3 (3.25 mm) needles, cast on 9 sts.

Row 1: Knit to end.

Row 2: K2, P5, K2.

Repeat last 2 rows, 3 more times.

Row 9: K3, Sl2, K1, psso, K3 (7 sts).

Row 10: K2, P3, K2.

Row 11: K2, Sl2, K1, psso, K2 (5 sts).

Row 12: K2, P1, K2.

Row 13: K2, M1, K1, M1, K2 (7 sts).

Row 14: Repeat row 10.

Row 15: K2, M1, K3, M1, K2 (9 sts).

Row 16: Repeat row 2.

Row 17: Repeat row 1.

Repeat last 2 rows, 3 more times.

Bind off.

BEADED BOW

Thread 20 beads onto the yarn. Cast on 9 sts.

Row 1: K1,* B1, K1, rep from * to end.

Row 2: K2, P5, K2.

Row 3: K2,* B1, K1, rep from *twice more, K1.

Row 4: Repeat row 2.

Row 5: K3, *B1, K1, rep from * once more, K2.

Row 6: Repeat row 2.

Row 7: K4, B1, K4.

Row 8: Repeat row 2.

Work as given for plain bow until row 17.

Row 17: Repeat row 7.

Row 18: Repeat row 2.

Row 19: Repeat row 5.

Row 20: Repeat row 2.

Row 21: Repeat row 3.

Row 22: Repeat row 2.
Row 23: Repeat row 1.
Bind off.

ASSEMBLY

Weave in all loose ends then block and press gently.
Cut a small strip of felt long enough to fit around the center of the bow and overlap slightly.

Stitch into position.
Next attach the hairpin to the wrong side of the bow—with the loop of the pin toward the center of the bow. Secure the pin to the bow by working a few backstitches around the back leg of the pin and into the felt fabric.

crown

Now anyone can be king or queen of the castle! The crown is knitted in one long garter-stitch strip using a smaller needle than usual to help the work keep its shape; the peaks are created using a simple increasing technique and then binding off.

Using 1 strand each of yarns A and B together throughout, cast on 5 sts.
Row 1: Knit to end.
Row 2: K4, yo, K1 (6 sts).
Row 3: Knit to end.
Row 4: K5, yo, K1 (7 sts).
Row 5: Knit to end.
Row 6: K6, yo, K1 (8 sts).
Row 7: Knit to end.
Row 8: K7, yo, K1 (9 sts).
Row 9: Knit to end.
Row 10: K8, yo, K1 (10 sts).
Row 11: Bind off 5 sts, knit to end (5 sts).

Repeat rows 2–11 until you have 10 peaks. On the last peak bind off all the sts.

ASSEMBLY

Sew the cast-on edge and the last five stitches from the final bound-off edge together to form the crown.

tip

To make the crown smaller reduce the number of peaks; if you want to make the crown larger simply add more repeats.

MATERIALS

Rowan Creative Focus Worsted (75% wool, 25% alpaca, approx. 220 yd/ 200 m per 3½ oz/100 g ball),
A shade 0802 Alpine

Rowan Shimmer 4 ply (60% cupro, 40% polyester, approx. 191 yd/175 m per 1 oz/25 g ball),
B shade 092 Silver

EQUIPMENT

1 pair size US 9 (5.5 mm) knitting needles

GAUGE

Approx. 13 sts x 22 rows = 4 in (10 cm) in garter stitch

FINISHED SIZE

Approx. 20 in (50 cm) long, to fit average adult

catnip mouse

Have hours of fun driving your cat crazy with this knitted mouse. The simple shape is filled with polyester toy stuffing and a pouch of catnip. The extra-long tail means you can hold on to the toy and play to your heart's content, keeping your hands out of harm's way.

BODY

Using yarn A and size US 3 (3.25 mm) needles, cast on 19 sts.

Starting with a knit row, work in stockinette stitch for 20 rows.

Row 21: K4, K2tog, (K1, K2tog) 3 times, K4 (15 sts).

Starting with a purl row, work 3 rows of stockinette stitch.

Row 25: K3, (K2tog) twice, K1, (K2tog) twice, K3 (11 sts).

Starting with a purl row, work 3 rows of stockinette stitch.

Row 29: K2, K2tog, Sl2 knitwise, K1, psso, K2tog, K2 (7 sts).

Break off yarn A, leaving a long enough length to sew body, join yarn B.

Row 30: Purl to end.

Row 31: K1, K2tog, K1, K2tog, K1 (5 sts).

Row 32: Purl to end.

Row 33: K1, Sl2 knitwise, K1, psso, K1 (3 sts).

Break off yarn and pull through 3 sts on needle.

EARS *make 2*

Using size US 3 (3.25 mm) needles and yarn A, cast on 9 sts.

Row 1: K8, turn.

Next row: Sl1, P5, turn.

Next row: Sl1, K4, turn.

Next row: Sl1, P3, turn.

Next row: Sl1, K2, turn.

Next row: Sl1, P1, turn.

Next row: Knit to end.

Next row: P1, P2tog, P3tog, P2tog, P1 (5 sts).

Break off yarn, slip stitches onto yarn, and pull tight—leaving a long enough length to sew ear to body.

TAIL

Using size US 3 (3.25 mm) needles, cast on 45 sts, and then bind off knitwise.

If you want to make the tail longer, cast on more stitches, then bind them all off.

ASSEMBLY

Weave in all loose ends of the gray yarn, and then sew edges together using mattress stitch from the nose down toward the cast-on edge. Leave cast-on edge open.

Cut out circle from cotton fabric, place teaspoon of catnip into center of fabric, run a thread around the outer edge of the circle, and pull tight. If you want to add more catnip do so at this point.

Tie the ends of the thread together to secure the top.

MATERIALS

Rowan Pure Wool DK (100% pure new wool, approx. 137 yd/125 m per 1¾ oz/ 50 g ball)
A shade 004 Anthracite

Rowan Handknit Cotton (100% cotton, approx. 88 yd/80 m per 1¾ oz/ 50 g ball)
B shade 303 Sugar

Rowan Siena 4-ply (100% cotton, approx. 126 yd/115 m per 1¾ oz/50g ball)
C shade 845 Shell

4-in (10-cm) square of cotton fabric to enclose catnip

Loose-leaf catnip

Thread

Toy stuffing

Small amount of black yarn for eyes

Small amount of gray yarn for whiskers

EQUIPMENT

1 pair size US 3 (3.25 mm) knitting needles

Tapestry needle

Sharp sewing needle

GAUGE

Approx. 25 sts x 32 rows = 4 in (10 cm) in stockinette stitch

Next insert stuffing into nose and head, place pouch of catnip into body, then fill the body with stuffing until you are happy with the shape.

Next using an end of gray yarn and tapestry needle, starting at the seam, run the yarn in and out of the stitches around the cast-on edge. Pull the yarn tight to close the opening, tie the ends of yarn together, then weave in the loose ends.

Next attach ears to head, weave in loose end from cast-on edge, then using the picture as guide, pin and stitch into position.

Next attach the tail—stitch it into position using the ends left from cast on and bind off.

Work 2 French knots for eyes using black thread—work 1 at each side of head.

Place whiskers at nose—cut 3 lengths of gray yarn, thread tapestry needle with 1 end, and insert through nose. Repeat for the other length of yarn.

Knot the whiskers together at the nose to secure.

rolled flower hairband

Stand out from the crowd in this decorative floral hairband. With a contrasting two-tone bound-off edge and large glass beads in the center, you'll want to have a different one for every day of the

Using yarn A and size US 3 (3.25 mm) needles, cast on 22 sts.

Row 1: Purl to end.

Row 2: K1, * Kfb, rep from * to last sts, K1 (42 sts).

Row 3: Purl to end.

Row 4: Repeat row 2 (82 sts).

Row 5: Purl to end.

Row 6: K31, change to yarn B, knit to end—do not break off yarn A.

Row 7: Bind off 51 sts in yarn B, bind off remaining sts in yarn A.

Weave in loose ends.

ASSEMBLY

Roll the right-hand side of flower at the cast-on edge up toward the change of color—pin to secure then stitch the base of the flower together. Repeat this process with the other end of the flower.

Sew the glass beads to the centers of the flowers.

Thread the cord elastic through the base of the flowers, then knot the ends together to make the hairband required size. Snip off excess elastic.

MATERIALS

Rowan Cotton Glace (100% cotton, approx. 127 yd/116 m per 1¾ oz/50 g ball)
A shade 841 Garnet

Rowan Panama (55% viscose, 33% cotton, 12% linen, approx. 148 yd/135 m per 1¾ oz/50 g ball)
B shade 308 Jacaranda

2 large glass beads

Approx. 6 in (15 cm) cord elastic

EQUIPMENT

1 pair size US 3 (3.25 mm) knitting needles

Tapestry needle

GAUGE

Approx. 23 sts x 32 rows = 4 in (10 cm) in stockinette stitch

covered hairclip

Whether you have long or short hair, this covered hairclip is a must-have accessory; it will brighten up any bad hair day. The clip is covered using a felt fabric slip, decorated with a simple piece of knitted fabric, and finished with a covered button.

Using size US 6 (4 mm)
  needles, cast on 11 sts.
Row 1: Purl to end.
Row 2: K1, * Kfb, rep from * to
  last st, K1.
Row 3: Purl to end.
Row 4: Repeat row 2.
Row 5: Purl to end.
Row 6: K1, * Kfb, rep from * to
  last st, K2.
Row 7: Purl to end.
Row 8: K1, * Kfb, rep from * to
  last st, K13.
Row 9: Purl to end.
Row 10: Knit to end.
Using tapestry needle, slip sts
  from knitting needle onto
  length of yarn and pull tight.
Break off yarn leaving long
  enough length to sew up
  side seam.
Sew up side seam using
  mattress stitch.

SLIP COVER FOR HAIRCLIP

Place clip on felt fabric then
  draw around outer edge.
Cut out 2 pieces to match
  shape of clip.
Draw a line along the top of 1
  piece (approx. 1 in/2 cm) then
  cut across—this will be the
  underside of clip cover.
Place 2 felt pieces together.
  Matching up the bottom
  edges of felt pieces, sew
  together around the
  outer edge.

FINISHING

Cover the metal button as per
  instructions.
Place in center of knitted
  section and sew together.
Place button and knitted
  section on felt clip cover and
  set into place.

MATERIALS

Rowan Kid Silk Haze (70%
super kid mohair, 30% silk,
approx. 230 yd/210 m per
1 oz/25 g ball)
1 x shade 579 Splendour
1 x 4-in (10-cm) hairclip
1 sheet black felt
1 x 1-in (2-cm) metal button
Cotton fabric to cover button

EQUIPMENT

1 pair size US 6 (4 mm)
knitting needles
Tapestry needle
Sharp sewing needle

bunting

These pretty flags are quick and simple to make. Start at the top and decrease all the way to create the flag shape. Add a two-row stripe sequence or duplicate stitch to create the pattern; these cheery designs are a great way of using up all your bits and pieces of yarn.

BASIC FLAG

Cast on 21 sts.

Rows 1–4: Knit.

Row 5: Knit to end.

Row 6: K2, purl to last 2 sts, K2.

Repeat last 2 rows once more.

Row 9: K2, K2togtbl, knit to last 4 sts, K2tog, K2 (19 sts).

Row 10: Repeat row 6.

Row 11: Repeat row 5.

Row 12: Repeat row 6.

Repeat rows 9–12 4 more times (11 sts).

Row 29: Repeat row 9 (9 sts).

Row 30: Repeat row 6.

Repeat last 2 rows once more (7 sts).

Next row: K2, Sl2 knitwise, K1, psso, K2 (5 sts).

Next row: K2, P1, K2.

Next row: K1, Sl2 knitwise, K1, psso, K1 (3 sts).

Next row: Knit to end.

Next row: K3tog.

Break off yarn and thread through st.

STRIPED FLAG

Work the first 4 rows in main color, work a 2-row stripe until 5 sts remain, then work in main color to end.

Stripe 1: yarns A and B.

Stripe 2: yarns D and E.

Stripe 3: yarns G and F.

PATTERNED FLAG

Work flag in one shade, then using duplicate stitch technique, work in desired pattern.

ASSEMBLY

Weave in loose ends, then block and press to correct size.

Roll out a length of tape and place your first flag approx 8 in (20 cm) from the end. Pin the flag onto the tape, then lay out the rest of the flags approx ¾ in (2 cm) apart along the tape. Once you are happy with the mix of colors, pin them into position.

Turn the bunting over so the wrong side is facing you, and then using a sharp sewing needle and thread to match tape, sew the tape to the flags using either a backstitch or hem stitch.

MATERIALS

Rowan Handknit Cotton DK (100% cotton, approx. 88 yd /80 m per 1¾ oz/50 g ball)
A shade 303 Sugar
B shade 215 Rosso
C shade 346 Atlantic
D shade 219 Gooseberry
E shade 354 Sunshine
F shade 251 Ecru
G shade 335 Thunder

½-in (1-cm) width tape or similar to stitch flags onto (equired length will depend on the number of flags)

Thread to match tape

EQUIPMENT

1 pair size US 6 (4 mm) knitting needles

Sharp sewing needle

GAUGE

Approx. 20 sts x 28 rows = 4 in (10 cm) in stockinette stitch

◄ projects

small cat pillow

This charming pillow is a must-have addition to any room. The shape is created using a mix of intarsia and decreasing techniques. Embellish it with a few lines of embroidery and felt fabric eyes and nose.

Use 2 strands of yarn together throughout—take one end from inside and one end from outside and use together.

Using size US 10½ (6.5 mm) needles and yarn B, cast on 23 sts.

Work from graph using intarsia technique until row 31.

Shape for ears as follows.

Next row: K1, K2togtbl, knit until 6 sts on right hand needle, turn.

Work on these 6 sts only.

**Next row: Purl to end

Next row: K3, K2tog, K1 (5 sts).

Next row: Purl to end.

Next row: K1, Sl1, K2tog, psso, K1 (3 sts).

Next row: Purl to end.

Next row: K3tog.

Break off yarn and pull through stitch on needle.

Rejoin yarn to remaining stitches.

Next row: K1, K2togtbl, knit to 3 sts, K2tog, K1 (6 sts).

Work as given for 1st ear working from **.

FINISHING

Weave in all loose ends, then block and press fabric.

Using 2 strands of yarn B and picture as guide, work 1 vertical row of duplicate stitch at the center of the cream portion of cat to create legs.

Again using 2 strands of yarn B and picture as guide, work a row of backstitch from right to left in a slight curve to create head.

ASSEMBLY

Cut out felt fabric backing to match knitted section of cat, then cut out 2 lozenge shapes from green for eyes, and small triangle with rounded edges from pink for nose.

Then, using picture as guide, pin and stitch eyes and nose to face. Work satin stitch vertically to make the center of the eyes.

Next pin the backing to the wrong side of the knitted fabric and stitch around using sharp sewing needle and gray thread.

Insert stuffing from bottom—use knitting needle to push up into the corners of the ears.

Once you are happy with the amount of stuffing sew up the base of cat.

MATERIALS

Rowan Kid Classic (70% lambswool, 22% kid mohair, 8% polyamide, approx. 153 yd/140 m per 1¾ oz/ 50g ball)
A shade 828 Feather
B shade 831 Smoke

1 sheet gray felt fabric for backing

1 small square green felt fabric for eyes

1 small square pink felt fabric for nose

Thread to match felt colors

Toy stuffing

EQUIPMENT

1 x pair size US 10½ (6.5 mm) knitting needles

Tapestry needle

Sharp sewing needle

Glass-headed pins

GAUGE

Approx. 15 sts x 20 rows

= 4 in (10 cm) in stockinette stitch

FINISHED SIZE

Approx. 5 in x 7½ in (13 cm x 19 cm)

GRAPH AND TEMPLATE

See pages 122 and 125

lion

Make the most of textural knitting with this little big cat. The loopy knit stitch is just perfect for this project. The simple use of color and embellishments give this Leo his finishing touches.

MANE

Using size US 6 (4 mm) needles and yarn A, cast on 29 sts.

Row 1: Knit to end.

Row 2 (WS): K1, * loop 1, K1, rep from * to end.

Row 3: K1, * K2tog, K1, rep from * to end (20 sts).

Row 4: K1, * loop 1, K1, rep from * to last sts, K1.

Row 5: K2, * K2tog, K1, rep from * to end (14 sts).

Row 6: Knit to end.

Row 7: P1, * P2tog, rep from * to last st, P1.

Bind off.

FACE

Using size US 3 (3.25 mm) needles and yarn C, cast on 38 sts.

Row 1 (WS): Purl to end.

Change to yarn B.

Row 2: K1, * K2tog, K2, rep from * to last st, K1 (29 sts).

Row 3: Purl to end.

Row 4: K1, * K2tog, K1, rep from * to last st, K1 (20 sts).

Row 5: Purl to end.

Row 6: K1, * K2tog, rep from * to last st, K1 (11 sts).

Row 7: Purl to end.

Break off yarn and pull through sts on needle—leave long enough length to sew side seam.

ASSEMBLY

Weave in loose ends, and then gently block and press face section.

Next sew side seam of mane section—leaving a space at the center for inserting stuffing.

Place the face section to the center of the mane section and sew into position.

Cut 2 small ear shapes from brown felt, then using picture as guide, sew into position on the brown section of the face.

FINISHING

Next cut small circular section of felt for nose and sew into position at center of the face. Using picture as guide, embroider the face using black yarn.

Insert small amount of stuffing through the opening in the mane section.

Cut circle of felt to match back of mane section, then stitch it into position.

MATERIALS

Rowan Creative Focus Worsted (75% wool, 25% alpaca, approx. 220 yd/200 m per 3½ oz/100 g ball)
A shade 3810 Saffron

Rowan Fine Tweed 4-ply (100% wool, approx. 98 yd/90 m per 1 oz/25 g ball)
B shade 383 Leyburn
C shade 363 Keld

4-in (10-cm) square brown felt fabric for backing, nose, and ears

Small amount of black yarn for face

Toy stuffing

Brown thread

EQUIPMENT

1 pair size US 6 (4 mm) knitting needles

1 pair size US 3 (3.25 mm) knitting needles

Tapestry needle

Sharp sewing needle

broad strap booties

These booties would make the perfect gift for any newborn. They are knitted from the sole up to the bound-off edge, and the toe shaping is created using straightforward short row shaping technique.

BOOTIE *make 2*

Using size US 3 (3.25 mm) needles and yarn A, cast on 29 sts.

Row 1: Knit to end.

Row 2: K1, yo, K13, yo, K1, yo, K13, yo, K1 (33 sts).

Row 3: Knit to end—knit into back of yo's on this and every following row.

Row 4: K2, yo, K13, yo, K3, yo, K13, yo, K2 (37 sts).

Row 5: Knit to end.

Row 6: K3, yo, K13, yo, K5, yo, K13, yo, K3 (41 sts).

Row 7: Knit to end.

Row 8: K4, yo, K13, yo, K7, yo, K13, yo, K4 (45 sts).

Next work 6 rows in garter stitch ending with a WS row.

Break off yarn A and join yarn B.

Starting with a knit row work 2 rows in stockinette stitch.

Shape toe as follows:

Next row: K28, K2togtbl, turn.

Next row: Sl1, P9, Ptog, turn.

Next row: Sl1, K9, K2togtbl, knit to end.

Next row: Purl to end (42 sts).

Break off yarn B, change to yarn A.

Next row: K15, K2tog, K1, K2tog, K2, K2togtbl, K1, K2togtbl, K15 (38 sts).

Next row: Knit to end.

Next row: Bind off 24, K2 (3 sts on right hand needle), bind off rest of row.

Break off yarn.

STRAP

Go back to 3 sts on needle and knit approx. 14 rows in garter stitch.

Bind off.

ASSEMBLY

Sew the bound-off edge of strap to the other side of the booties.

Sew up back seam and sole.

MATERIALS

Rowan Handknit Cotton DK (100% cotton, approx. 93 yd/85 m per 50g ball)
A shade 349 Ochre
B shade 303 Sugar

EQUIPMENT

1 pair size US 3 (3.25 mm) knitting needles

Tapestry needle

GAUGE

Approx. 22 sts x 30 rows = 4 in (10 cm) in stockinette stitch

FINISHED SIZE

To fit 0–6-month-old baby

sheep fridge magnet

For those of us that are wool-mad, this makes a great decoration… Made up of two loopy knit textured circles, the fabric is fluffed up by felting slightly, which adds to the effect.

BODY

Using size US 2 (2.75 mm) needles, cast on 47 sts.
Row 1: Knit to end.
Row 2: K1, * loop 1, K1, rep from * to end.
Row 3: K1, * K2tog, K3, rep from * to last sts, K1 (38 sts).
Row 4: K1, * loop 1, K1, rep from * to last st, K1.
Row 5: K1, * K2tog, K2, rep from * to last sts, K1 (29 sts).
Row 6: Repeat row 2.
Row 7: K1, * K2tog, K1, rep from * to last sts, K1 (20 sts).
Row 8: Repeat row 4.
Row 9: K1, * K2tog, rep from * to last sts, K1 (11 sts).
Row 10: Repeat row 2.
Break off yarn, leaving 16 in (40 cm). Slip stitches on needle onto thread and pull tight.
Sew up side seam to form circular body.

HEAD

Using size US 2 (2.75 mm) needles, cast on 20 sts.
Row 1: Knit to end.
Row 2: K1, * loop 1, K1, rep from * to last st, K1.
Row 3: K1, * K2tog, rep from * to last sts, K1 (11 sts).
Row 4: K1, * loop 1, K1, rep from * to end.
Row 5: K1, * K2tog, rep from *

to last 2 sts, K2 (7 sts).
Row 6: Repeat row 2.
Break off yarn, leaving 12 in (30 cm). Slip stitches on needle onto thread and pull tight.
Sew side seam to form head.

FINISHING

Weave in all loose ends on head and body.
Put on your rubber gloves.
Place fabric in a basin with a small amount of cold water and a dash of detergent.
Make sure the fabric has soaked up the cold water.
Rub the fabric between your hands, agitating in a circular motion—you will see the felting process start.
Next, throw the fabric into the basin approx. 20–30 times—this helps shock the fibers and felt them together.
Once fabric is suitably felted, run the fabric under the tap to remove the soapy liquid.

MATERIALS

Rowan 4-ply Fine Tweed (100% wool, approx. 98 yd/90 m per 1 oz/ 25 g ball)
1 x shade 376 Bell busk
1 sheet black felt fabric
Black thread
1 sew-on fridge magnet

EQUIPMENT

1 pair size US 2 (2.75 mm) knitting needles
Tapestry needle
Rubber gloves
Detergent
Towel
Pins
Sharp sewing needle

TEMPLATE

See page 125

Once you are happy with it, pour a kettle of boiling water over the fabric and into the basin, taking care to avoid splashing yourself with the boiling water.

Swish the fabric around and again pick up (taking care as it will be hot), squeeze out water, and agitate between your hands—repeat this last process.

Lay fabric on a towel, fold the towel over, covering up the fabric, then roll up.

Squeeze the towel to help remove excess water from the fabric.

Remove fabric from towel—gently pull out into sheep shapes, then let dry.

Next, using templates on page 125, cut out face section for head, then cut out legs, tail, and body section.

Using picture as guide, pin and stitch face to center of head, and then sew head into position on the body.

Next pin and sew legs and tail to wrong side of body section.

Sew magnet to the center of the right side of the felt body section, then place body section on the back of the knitted body with magnet to the outside and sew into position.

crossover booties

This design is a new take on a simple bootie pattern, worked in two halves in contrasting colors to emphasize the crossover design. The button fastening adds that special extra something.

SOLE *make 2*

Using yarn A and size US 3 (3.25 mm) needles, cast on 30 sts.

Row 1: K1, yo, K13, yo, K1, yo, K1, yo, K13, yo, K1 (35 sts).

Row 2: K1, Ktbl, K13, Ktbl, K1, Ktbl, K1, Ktbl, K13, Ktbl, K1.

Row 3: K2, yo, K13, yo, K2, yo, K3, yo, K13, yo, K2 (40 sts).

Row 4: K2, Ktbl, K13, Ktbl, K3, Ktbl, K2, Ktbl, K13, Ktbl, K2.

Row 5: K3, yo, K13, yo, K4, yo, K4, yo, K13, yo, K3 (45 sts).

Row 6: K3, Ktbl, K13, Ktbl, K4, Ktbl, K4, Ktbl, K13, Ktbl, K3.

TOP SECTION OF BOOTIE

(worked in 2 halves to create crossover)

Row 1: K28, turn. Place remaining stitches on stitch holder or waste yarn.

Row 2: K2, purl to end.

Repeat the last 2 rows once more.

Shape toe as follows:

Row 5: K24, K2tog, K2.

Next row: K2, P6, P2tog, turn.

Next row: Sl1, K4, K2tog, K2.

Next row: K2, P5, P2tog, turn.

Next row: Sl1, K3, K2tog, K2

Next row: K2, P4, P2tog, turn.

Next row: Sl1, K2, K2tog, K2.

MATERIALS

Rowan Handknit Cotton DK (100% cotton, approx. 93 yd/85 m per ball)
A shade 349 Ochre
B shade 352 Sea foam

2 small buttons

EQUIPMENT

1 pair size US 3 (3.25 mm) knitting needles

Tapestry needle

Stitch holder or waste yarn

GAUGE

Approx. 22 sts x 30 rows = 4 in (10 cm) in stockinette stitch

Next row: K2, P3, P2tog, turn.
Next row: Sl1, K1, K2tog, K2.
Next row: K2, P2, P2tog, turn.
Next row: Sl1, K2tog, K2.
Next row: K2, P2tog, turn.
Next row: Sl1, K3.
Next row: K2, P3tog, turn.
Next row: Sl1, K2.
Next row: K2, P2tog.
Repeat the last 2 rows until 3 sts remain on the needle, ending with K2, P2tog row.
Bind off as follows:
Sl1, K1, psso, K1, psso.
Break off yarn and thread through last stitch.

OTHER SIDE OF BOOTIE

Using yarn B, cast on 11 sts.
Row 1: K11. Replace held stitches on needle, right side facing you. Working from the toe of the bootie to the heel, knit to end (28 sts).
Row 2: P26, K2.
Repeat the last 2 rows once more.
Shape toe as follows:
Next row: K2, Sl1, K1, psso, K5, K2togtbl, turn.

Next row: Sl1, P6, K2.
Next row: K2, Sl1, K1, psso, K4, K2togtbl, turn.
Next row: Sl1, P5, K2.
Next row: K2, Sl1, K1, psso, K3, K2togtbl, turn.
Next row: Sl1, P4, K2.
Next row: K2, Sl1, K1, psso, K2, K2togtbl, turn.
Next row: Sl1, P3, K2.
Next row: K2, Sl1, K1, psso, K1, K2togtbl, turn.
Next row: Sl1, P2, K2.
Next row: K2, Sl1, K1, psso, K2togtbl, turn.
Next row: Sl1, P1, K2.
Next row: K2, Sl1, K2togtbl, psso, turn.
Next row: Sl1, K2.
Next row: K2, K2togtbl, turn.
Repeat the last 2 rows until 3 sts remain on the needle, ending with K2, K2togtbl row.
Bind off as follows:
Sl1, K1, psso, K1, psso.
Break off yarn and thread through last stitch.
Work 2nd bootie as the first, reversing the colors.

ASSEMBLY

Sew the back seam and sole using mattress stitch.
Next, using picture as guide, sew the cast-on toe stitches to the inside of one bootie and to the outside of the other bootie for the crossover.
Next sew a small button to the contrast color and sew a small amount of yarn to match on the other side for the loop.

baby mittens

These baby mittens are a modern take on a traditional pattern. The chevron lace border is worked in a contrasting two-row stripe. The mittens are knitted in a soft 100 percent cotton yarn, but could easily be knitted in a suitable DK-weight wool blend. Play around with color combinations—why not coordinate either the broad strap or crossover booties to make a matching set?

MATERIALS

Rowan Handknit Cotton DK (100% cotton, approx. 93 yd/85 m per ball)
A shade 349 Ochre
B shade 352 Sea foam

Satin ribbon (½ in/1 cm wide), approx. 8 in (20 cm) per mitten

EQUIPMENT
1 pair size US 3 (3.25 mm) knitting needles

Tapestry needle

GAUGE
Approx. 22 sts x 30 rows = 4 in (10 cm) in stockinette stitch

FINISHED SIZE
Approx. 2 in (5 cm) wide, 4 in (10 cm) long

MITTENS *make 2*

Using size US 3 (3.25 mm) needles and yarn A, cast on 22 sts.

Work 2 rows in garter stitch.

Change to yarn B.

Work 2 rows in stockinette stitch.

Change to yarn A.

Row 5: * K1, K2tog, K2, yo, K1, yo, K2 K2togtbl, K1 , rep from * once more.

Row 6: Purl to end.

Change to yarn B.

Row 7: Repeat row 5.

Row 8: Repeat row 6.

Change to yarn A.

Row 9: Repeat row 5.

Row 10: Repeat row 6.

Break off yarn A and change to yarn B.

Place eyelets.

Row 11: K1, * K2tog, yo, rep from * to last st, K1.

Row 12: Purl to end.

Starting with a knit row, work 10 rows in stockinette stitch.

Shape top.

Row 19: * K1, K2togtbl, K5, K2tog, K1, rep from * once more (18 sts).

Row 20: Purl to end.

Row 21: * K1, K2togtbl, K3, K2tog, K1, rep from * once more (14 sts).

Row 22: Purl to end.

Row 23: * K1, K2togtbl, K1, K2tog, K1, rep from * once more (10 sts).

Row 24: Purl to end.

ASSEMBLY

Next row: K5.

Fold knitting in half with wrong sides together; bind off using 3-needle method.

Break off yarn, leaving long enough length to sew side seam.

Block and press mittens.

With right side facing and using mattress stitch technique, sew side seams.

FINISHING

Cut satin ribbon in half—thread through eyelets.

Venetian mask

You shall go to the ball with this Venetian-inspired knitted mask. The mask is knitted from the center out toward the edge and will be completed within 30 minutes. The finishing off will take slightly longer, but it's worth it.

MASK *worked in 2 parts*

Using size US 3 (3.25 mm) needles, cast on 9 sts.

Row 1: Knit to end.

Row 2: Purl to end.

Row 3: K8, M1, K1 (10 sts).

Row 4: P9, M1, K1 (11 sts).

Row 5: K10, M1, K1 (12 sts).

Place eye.

Next row: P5.

Work on these 5 sts only, slip other sts onto stitch holder or spare needle if desired.

Next row: K4, M1, K1 (6 sts).

Next row: P6.

Next row: K5, M1, K1 (7 sts).

Next row: P7.

Next row: K1, K2togtbl, K4 (6 sts).

Next row: P6.

Next row: K1, M1, K5 (7 sts).

Next row: P7.

Next row: K4, K2tog, K1 (6 sts).

Next row: P6, M1, P1 (7 sts).

Next row: K7.

Next row: P7, M1, P1 (8 sts).

Next row: K8.

Next row: P7, M1, P1 (9 sts).

Break off yarn and rejoin to sts to work the other side of the eye.

With WS facing:

Next row: Bind off 2 sts, P4, M1, P1 (6 sts).

Next row: K6.

Next row: P1, P2tog, P2, M1, P1 (6 sts).

Next row: K6.

Next row: P5, M1, P1 (7 sts).

Next row: K4, K2tog, K1 (6 sts).

Next row: P5, M1, P1 (7 sts).

Next row: K7.

Next row: P7.

Next row: K7.

Next row: P7.

Next row: K1, M1, K6 (8 sts).

Next row: P8.

Next row: K8.

Next row: P8.

Join both pieces together.

K7, M1 K1, knit across all sts to end (18 sts).

Next row: P1, P2tog, P15 (17 sts).

Next row: K1, K2togthl, K to end (16 sts).

Next row: P1, P2tog, P to end (15 sts).

Next row: Knit to end.

Next row: P1, P2tog, P to end (14 sts).

Next row: K1, K2togtbl, K to last 3 sts, K2tog, K1 (12 sts).

MATERIALS

Rowan Cotton Glace (100% cotton, approx 127 yd/116 m per 1¾ oz/50 g ball)
1 x shade 727 Black

Cardboard

Thick cardboard

1 rectangle of black felt 9 in x 12 in (23 cm x 30 cm)

Black thread

Gold trim

Approx. 6 in (15 cm) cord elastic

EQUIPMENT

1 pair size US 3 (3.25 mm) knitting needles

Stitch holder/spare needle

Tailor's chalk

Sharp scissors

Double-sided sticky tape

Tapestry needle

Sharp sewing needle

GAUGE

Approx. 25 sts x 32 rows = 4 in (10 cm) in stockinette stitch

TEMPLATE

See page 125

◄ projects

Next row: P1, P2tog, P to end (11 sts).

Next row: K to last 3 sts, K2tog, K1 (10 sts).

Next row: P1, P2tog, P to last st, M1, P1 (10 sts).

Next row: Knit to end.

Next row: Bind off 3 sts, P to end (7 sts).

Next row: Knit to end.

Next row: Bind off 3 sts, K to last st, M1, K1 (5 sts).

Next row: K2, K2tog, K1 (4 sts).

Next row: P1, P2tog, P1 (3 sts).

Next row: K1, K2tog (2 sts).

Next row: K2tog.

Break off yarn and slip through st on needle, pull tight to secure.

With right side facing pick up 9 sts along cast-on edge and work the other side of mask as follows:

Row 1: Purl to end.

Row2: K1, M1, knit to end (10 sts).

Row 3: P1, M1, purl to end (11 sts).

Row 4: K1, M1, knit to end (12 sts).

Row 5: P1, M1, P4, turn.

Place eye.

Work on these 6 sts only, slip other sts onto stitch holder or spare needle if desired.

Next row: K6.

Next row: P1, M1, P2, P2tog, P1 (6 sts).

Next row: K6.

Next row: P1, M1, P5 (7 sts).

Next row: K1, K2tog, K4 (6 sts).

Next row: P1, M1, P5 (7 sts).

Next row: Knit to end.

Next row: Purl to end.

Next row: Knit to end.

Next row: Purl to end.

Next row: K6, M1, K1 (8 sts).

Next row: Purl to end.

Next row: Knit to end.

Next row: Purl to end.

Break off yarn and rejoin to sts to work the other side of the eye.

Next row: Bind off 2 sts, purl to end (5 sts).

Next row: K1, M1, K4 (6 sts).

Next row: P6.

Next row: K1, M1, K5 (7 sts).

Next row: P7.

Next row: K4, K2tog, K1 (6 sts).

Next row: P6.

Next row: K5, M1, K1 (7 sts).

Next row: P7.

Next row: K1, K2togtbl, K4 (6 sts).

Next row: P1, M1, P5 (7 sts).

Next row: K7.

Next row: P1, M1, P6 (8 sts).

Next row: K8.

Next row: P1, M1, P7.

Join both pieces together.

Knit across all the stitches from both parts of mask as follows:

Next row: K8, M1, K to end (18 sts).

Next row: Purl to last 3 sts, P2tog, P1 (17 sts).

Next row: Knit to last 3 sts, K2tog, K1 (16 sts).

Next row: Purl to last 3 sts, P2tog, P1 (15 sts).

Next row: Knit to end.

Next row: Purl to last 3 sts, P2tog, P1 (14 sts).

Next row: K1, K2tog, K to last 3 sts, K2togtbl, K1 (12 sts).

Next row: Purl to last 3 sts, P2tog, P1 (11 sts).

Next row: K1, K2tog, knit to end
(10 sts).

Next row: P1, M1, purl to end
(11 sts).

Next row: Bind off 3 sts, knit to
end (8 sts).

Next row: Purl to end.

Next row: Bind off 3 sts, knit to
end (5 sts).

Next row: P1, M1, P1, P2tog, P1
(5 sts).

Next row: K1, K2tog, K to end
(4 sts).

Next row: P1, P2tog, P1 (3 sts).

Next row: K1, K2tog (2 sts).

Next row: P2tog.

Break off yarn and slip through
st on needle, pull tight to
secure.

ASSEMBLY

Weave in loose ends, then block
and press fabric.

Using template, cut out mask
shape from thick cardboard.

Next cut out mask shape in
black felt approx. ½ in (1.5 cm)
wider than cardboard.

Place cardboard on felt fabric
and draw around the outer
and inner edge of eyes with
tailor's chalk.

Next, using sharp scissors, snip

in toward the chalk line at
approx. ½ in (1 cm) intervals
around the outer edge, then
repeat this process for the
inner eyes.

These tabs will fold over the
cardboard and allow the felt
fabric to fit the shape snugly.

Next run pieces of double-sided
sticky tape around the eyes
and outer edge, then place
cardboard with sticky side up
on top of the felt fabric, fold
the tabs over, and press firmly
down onto the sticky tape.

Next, place the WS of knitted
piece down onto the
cardboard so it covers the tabs.

Next, using sharp sewing needle
and thread, sew around the
outer edge of mask, and then
sew around the eyes.

Sew the trim to the front knitted
part of the mask.

Then on the inside section
of the mask knot one end
of the elastic and thread
through into position, bring
it around the back of mask
and through the other side
to match. Knot the elastic,
making sure mask will sit
snugly on head.

leaf headband

Worked in a stunning cobalt blue, this headband will complement any hair color, and the bugle beads will catch the light beautifully.

SIDE LEAF

Work from stem upward.

Using size US 3 (3.25 mm) double-pointed needles, cast on 4 sts.

Work 4 rows I-cord.

Next row: K1, K2togtbl, K1 (3 sts).

Work 4 more rows of I-cord.

Make leaf as follows:

Cast on 8 sts using 2-needle method (11 sts).

**Next row: K8, turn.

Next row: Sl1, purl to end.

Next row: K6, turn.

Next row: Sl1, purl to end.

Next row: K4, turn.

Next row: Sl1, purl to end.

Next bind off 6 sts, K5, turn and cast on 8 sts using 2-needle cast on method.

Next row: P8, turn.

Next row: Sl1, knit to end.

Next row: P6, turn.

Next row: Sl1, knit to end.

Next row: P4, turn.

Next row: Sl1, knit to end.

Bind off 6 sts, P2—last st from bind off counts as one of these sts, P3tog, P2 (5 sts).

Cast on 7 sts using 2-needle cast on method.

Work from ** twice more casting on 7 sts instead of 8.

SHAPE TOP OF LEAF

Starting with a knit row, work 8 rows in stockinette stitch.

Next row: K1, Sl2, K1, psso, K1 (3 sts).

Next row: P3tog.

Break off yarn and thread through loop on needle, then pull tight to secure.

Weave in loose ends.

Block and press to flatten the leaf sections.

FINISHING

Using template, cut leaf shape from felt fabric.

Then pin and stitch to the purl side of the fabric using matching thread.

Next, using picture as guide, sew the bugle beads onto the front section of the knitted leaf.

COVER HEADBAND

Cut 3 or 4 strips approx. ¾ in (1.5 cm) wide from the felt fabric and sew together to form one long strip.

Holding the band, take the strip of felt fabric and wrap around the "leg" of the band in a spiral fashion—place a glass headed pin to secure the end of the strip.

Continue wrapping the fabric around the band, gently stretching so it fits snugly—do not pull tightly or strip will snap.

Thread sharp sewing needle with matching thread and, where the felt fabric has been held together with glass headed pin, secure using a backstitch or whipstitch.

Place leaf onto headband—pin into position then sew together working through all the layers.

flowers

Have beautiful little flowers all year round with this selection of knitted designs. Each of the flowers uses a different technique so they are great for expanding your knitting knowledge. Dip in and out of these patterns to make a whole bunch. Try using different weights or textures of yarn for a range of effects.

loopy flower

Using size US 3 (3.25 mm) needles and yarn A, cast on 100 sts.

Row 1: K2, *bind off 6 sts, K3 (4 sts on right-hand needle after bind-off), repeat from * to end, last rep ending K1 (40 sts).

Row 2: Purl to end.

Row 3: K2, *K2togtbl, K2tog, repeat from * to last 2 sts, K2 (22 sts).

Row 4: Purl to end.

Row 5: K1, * K2tog, rep from * to last sts, K1 (12 sts).

Break off yarn and thread through sts on needle, pull tight, and allow flower to roll up.

Secure yarn and base of flower by working a few stitches straight through the bottom.

Weave in loose ends.

STEM

Using size US 2 (3 mm) double-pointed needles and yarn B, cast on 4 sts.

Work I-cord for approx. 22 rows or until required length.

Next row: K1, M1 by picking up strand in between sts and working into the back, K2, M1, K1 (6 sts).

Next row: Purl to end.

Next row: K1, M1, K4, M1, K1 (8 sts).

Next row: Purl to end.

Next row: K1, M1, K6, M1, K1 (10 sts).

Next row: Purl to end.

Bind off, leaving long enough length to sew side seam.

FINISHING

Sew seam of flower base.

Pin the base of flower to the wrong side of the flat base. Sew into position.

Next cut length of craft wire to match length of stem—insert up through the center of the I-cord.

MATERIALS

Yarn: Rowan Cotton Glace (100% cotton, approx. 126 yd/115 m per 1¾ oz/ 50 g ball)

A shade 832 Persimmon

B shade 812 Ivy

18-gauge (1.2 mm) craft wire, approx. 8 in (20 cm) length

EQUIPMENT

1 pair size US 3 (3.25 mm) knitting needles

1 pair size US 2 (3 mm) double-pointed knitting needles

Pliers

GAUGE

Approx. 25 sts x 32 sts = 4 in (10 cm) in stockinette stitch

rounded-petal flower

FLOWER

Using size US 3 (3.25 mm) needles and yarn A, cast on 6 sts.

Row 1: Knit to end.

Row 2: Purl 4 sts, wrap next st as follows: bring yarn forward, slip next st, then bring yarn back, turn.

Row 3: Sl1, K3, M1, K1 (7 sts).

Repeat the last 2 rows twice more (9 sts).

Row 8: Purl to end picking up wrapped stitch strand and working together with stitch.

Row 9: K6, K2tog, K1 (8 sts).

Row 10: P5, wrap next st, turn.

Row 11: Sl1, K2, K2tog, K1.

Row 12: P3, wrap next st, turn.

Row 13: Sl1, K2, K2tog, K1.

Row 14: Purl to end picking up wrapped stitch strand and working together with stitch.

Repeat last 14 rows 5 more times.

STEM

Using size US 2 (3 mm) double-pointed needles and yarn B, cast on 4 sts.

Work I-cord for approx. 22 rows or until required length.

Next row: K1, M1 by picking up strand in between sts and working into the back, K2, M1, K1 (6 sts).

Next row: Purl to end.

Next row: K1, M1, K4, M1, K1 (8 sts).

Next row: Purl to end.

Next row: K1, M1, K6, M1, K1 (10 sts).

Next row: Purl to end.

Next row: K1, M1, K8, M1, K1 (12 sts).

Next row: Purl to end.

Bind off, leaving long enough length to sew side seam.

FINISHING

Block and gently press flower fabric.

Roll up flower at straight edge—use picture as guide.

Secure yarn and base of flower by working a few stitches straight through all the layers.

Weave in loose ends.

Sew seam of flower base.

Pin the base of flower to the wrong side of the flower base. Sew into position.

Next, cut length of craft wire to match length of stem—insert up through the center of the I-cord.

MATERIALS

Rowan Cotton Glace (100% cotton, approx. 126 yd/115 m per 1¾ oz/50 g ball)

A shade 841 Garnet

B shade 812 Ivy

18-gauge (1.2 mm) craft wire, approx. 8 in (20 cm) length

EQUIPMENT

1 pair size US 3 (3.25 mm) knitting needles

1 pair size US 2 (3 mm) double pointed needles

Pliers

GAUGE

Approx. 25 sts x 32 sts = 4 in (10 cm) in stockinette stitch

lace flower

FLOWER

Using size US 3 (3.25 mm) needles and yarn A, cast on 6 sts.

Row 1: K2, yo, K2tog, yo, knit to end (7 sts).

Row 2: P5, K2.

Row 3: K3, yo, K2tog, yo, knit to end (8 sts).

Row 4: P6, K2.

Row 5: K4, yo, K2tog, yo, knit to end (9 sts).

Row 6: P7, K2.

Row 7: K5, yo, K2tog, yo, knit to end (10 sts).

Row 8: P8, K2.

Row 9: K6, yo, K2tog, yo, knit to end (11 sts).

Row 10: Bind off 5 sts, purl to last 2 sts, K2 (6 sts).

Repeat rows 1–10 once more.

Rows 21–27: Repeat rows 1–7.

Row 28: Bind off 4 sts, purl to last 2 sts, K2 (6 sts).

Repeat rows 21–28 once more.

Rows 37–41: Repeat rows 1–5.

Row 42: Bind off 3 sts, purl to last 2 sts, K2 (6 sts).

Repeat rows 37–41 once more.

Bind off.

STEM

Using yarn B and size US 2 (3 mm) double-pointed needles, cast on 4 sts.

Work I-cord for approx. 22 rows or until required length.

Next row: K1, M1 by picking up strand in between sts and working into the back, K2, M1, K1 (6 sts).

Next row: Purl to end.

Next row: K1, M1, K4, M1, K1 (8 sts).

Next row: Purl to end.

Next row: K1, M1, K6, M1, K1 (10 sts).

Next row: Purl to end.

Next row: K1, M1, K8, M1, K1 (12 sts).

Next row: Purl to end.

Bind off, leaving long enough length to sew side seam.

FINISHING

Block and gently press lace flower fabric.

Roll up flower at straight edge.

Secure yarn and base of flower by working a few stitches straight through all the layers.

Weave in loose ends.

Pin the base of flower to the wrong side of the flat base. Sew into position.

Next cut length of craft wire to match length of stem—insert up through the center of the I-cord.

rosebud

FLOWER

Using size US 3 (3.25 mm) needles and yarn A, cast on 30 sts.

Row 1 (WS): Purl to end.

Work each petal on 10 sts as follows:

** Knit K9, yo, slip next st, yarn back, turn (wrap 1).

Slip next st, P7, wrap 1, turn.

Slip next st, K6, wrap 1, turn.

Slip next st, P5, wrap 1, turn.

Slip next st, K4, wrap 1, turn.

Slip next st, P3, wrap 1, turn.

Slip next st, K2, wrap 1, turn.

Slip next st, P1, wrap 1, turn.

Next, knit until you have 10 sts on RHN, picking up and knitting the wrapped stitches.

Repeat pattern from ** once more.

Next, knit until you have 20 sts on RHN, picking up and knitting the wrapped stitches.

Repeat pattern from ** once more. Knit to end, picking up and knitting the wrapped stitches.

Next row: Purl to end, picking up and knitting the wrapped stitches.

Next row: *K3, K2tog, K2togtbl, K3, repeat from * to end (24 sts).

Next row: *P3, P2tog, P3, rep from * to end (21 sts).

Next row: *K2, Sl2 knitwise, K1, psso, K2, rep from * to end (15 sts).

Next row: Knit to end.

Bind off.

STEM

Using size US 2 (3 mm) double-pointed needles and yarn B, cast on 4 sts.

Work I-cord for approx. 22 rows or until required length.

Next row: K1, M1 by picking up strand in between sts and working into the back, K2, M1, K1 (6 sts).

Next row: Purl to end.

Next row: K1, M1, K4, M1, K1 (8 sts).

Next row: Purl to end.

Next row: K1, M1, K6, M1, K1 (10 sts).

Next row: Purl to end.

Bind off, leaving long enough length to sew side seam.

FINISHING

Gently press cupped flower fabric with steam iron.

Roll up flower at straight edge, using picture as guide.

Secure yarn and base of flower by working a few stitches straight through all the layers.

Weave in loose ends.

Sew seam of slightly cupped base at top of stem.

Pin the base of flower to the wrong side of the slightly cupped base at top of stem. Sew into position.

Next cut length of craft wire to match length of stem and insert up through the center of the I-cord.

MATERIALS

Rowan Cotton Glace (100% cotton, approx. 126 yd/115 m per 1¾ oz/50 g ball)
A shade 741 Poppy
B shade 814 Shoot

18-gauge (1.2 mm) craft wire, approx. 8 in (20 cm) length

EQUIPMENT

1 pair size US 3 (3.25 mm) knitting needles

1 pair size US 2 (3 mm) double-pointed needles

Pliers

GAUGE

Approx. 25 sts x 32 sts = 4 in (10 cm) in stockinette stitch

strawberry charm

This charming strawberry shape is created using a mixture of increasing and decreasing techniques, with the beads placed along the way. Why not make a whole bunch of them, as the perfect summertime table decorations.

MATERIALS

Rowan Cotton Glace (100% cotton, approx. 126 yd/115 m per 1¾ oz/50 g ball)
1 x shade 741 Poppy

1 packet Debbie Abrahams 0/6 beads, color 36

Toy stuffing

1 x 4 in (10 cm) square of lime green felt fabric

1 x 4 in (10 cm) square of dark green felt fabric

Green sewing thread

EQUIPMENT

1 pair size US 3 (3.25 mm) knitting needles

Tapestry needle

Sharp sewing needle

GAUGE

Approx. 25 sts x 32 rows = 4 in (10 cm) in stockinette stitch

TEMPLATE

See page 124

Thread 30 beads onto to the yarn (see page 118).

With size US 3 (3.25 mm) needles, cast on 7 sts.

Row 1 (WS): Purl to end.

Row 2 (RS): K1,* M1, K1, rep from * to end (13 sts).

Row 3: Purl to end.

Row 4: K1,* M1, K1,B1, K1, M1, K1, rep from * to end (19 sts).

Row 5: Purl to end.

Row 6: K1*, M1, K5, M1, K1, rep from * to end (25 sts).

Row 7: Purl to end.

Row 8: K1,* M1, K1, B1, K3, B1, K1, M1, K1, rep from * to end (31 sts).

Row 9: Purl to end.

Row 10: K1*, M1, K9, M1, K1rep from * to end (37 sts).

Row 11: Purl to end.

Row 12: K1,* M1, K1, B1, K3, B1, K3, B1, K1, M1, K1, rep from * to end (43 sts).

Row 13: Purl to end.

Row 14: K1*, M1, K13, M1, K1, rep from * to end (49 sts).

Row 15: Purl to end.

Row 16: K1* K2, (B1, K3) 3 times, B1, K1 rep from * to end.

Starting and ending with a purl row work 3 rows in stockinette stitch.

Shape top.

Row20: K1, *K2togtbl, K4, Sl2 knitwise, K1, psso, K4, K2tog,

K1, rep from * to end (37 sts).

Starting and ending with a purl row work 3 rows in stockinette stitch.

Row 26: K1, *K2togtbl, K2, Sl2 knitwise, K1, psso, K2, K2tog, K1, rep from * to end (25 sts).

Row 27: Purl to end.

Row 28: K1, * K2togtbl, K3 K2tog, K1, rep from * to end (19 sts).

Row 29: Purl to end.

Row 30: K1,* Sl2 knitwise, K1, psso, K3, rep from * to end (13 sts).

Row 31: Purl to end.

Break off yarn and thread through stitches on needle, pull tight, and secure yarn.

ASSEMBLY

Neaten all loose ends on the wrong side of the fabric.

Gently press on the wrong side with a steam iron.

Using mattress stitch, sew half of the seam.

Insert enough stuffing to create the shape of the strawberry, and then finish off sewing the seam.

MAKING TOP

Cut a ½-in (1-cm) wide strip from lime green felt—fold in half to create a loop, then pin and stitch to the top of the strawberry.

Next, using template, cut leaves from dark green felt fabric. Cut circle at center of leaves to allow the loop to fit through.

Place leaves down over loop and into position at top of strawberry.

Sew leaves into position using green thread.

tea light decoration

This simple pattern makes a great decoration for dressing up a basic tea light and turning it into something special. The beads are placed toward the top edge of the open wire-knitted fabric, which will cast shadows when the tea light is lit.

Use 2 strands of wire together throughout.

Thread the beads onto the wire in color sequence A, B, C, D until all the beads have been used up.

If you want to change the sequence remember the first bead you thread on will be the last bead you use.

Using size US 6 (4 mm) needles, cast on 12 sts.

Row 1: Knit to end.

Row 2: Knit to end.

Row 3: (Bring bead up to needles and K1) twice, knit to end.

Row 4: K9 (bring bead up to needles and K1) twice, K1.

The last 2 rows form pattern.

Repeat until you have used up all the beads ending with row 4.

Bind off.

Next, holding the fabric between your fingers and thumb, run your fingers down the fabric to open it out.

Sew the cast-on and bound-off edges together allowing them to lap over slightly so the beads match up. Weave in the other loose end.

MATERIALS

I reel turquoise craft wire, 30-gauge (0.3 mm) thick

I reel silver craft wire, 30-gauge (0.3 mm) thick

Small glass beads, 11 each of dark green (A), lime green (B), yellow (C), and blue (D)

EQUIPMENT

I pair size US 6 (4 mm) knitting needles

Sharp sewing needle

FINISHED SIZE

Length approx. 5 in (13 cm), to fit average tea light

safety

The wire will get hot when the candle is lit. Don't pick up the decoration when lit, and never leave lit candles unattended.

cable coat hanger

Why not give your wardrobe an update of a different kind with this cable coat hanger cover? Knitted lengthwise in one long strip, it's a simple rib with a twist. The cover is worked in a light neutral shade to avoid any possible color transfer onto your clothes.

Using size US 6 (4 mm)
  needles, cast on 12 sts.
Row 1: P3, K6, P3.
Row 2: K3, P6, K3.
Repeat last 2 rows 3 more times.
Row 9: P3, C6B, P3.
Row 10: K3, P6, K3.
Row 11: P3, K6, P3.
Repeat last 2 rows 2 more times,
  then row 10 once more.
Next row: Repeat row 9.
Repeat the last 8 rows until 12
  cables have been completed.
Then repeat rows 10–11 3 more
  times, then row 10 once more.
Bind off.
Weave in loose ends.

COVER COAT HANGER
Cut length of felt fabric
  to match the length and
  circumference of hanger.
Make a slit halfway along the
  length (to match position of
  metal hook) and cut in toward
  the center of the fabric.
Place a strip of double-sided
  sticky tape lengthwise along
  the top of hanger. Place the
  fabric onto the sticky tape,
leaving a portion free for the
other edge of the fabric to stick
to, and wrap the felt fabric
around the hanger. If required
you can stitch the ends of the
felt fabric together.
Next unscrew the metal hook
  from hanger or, if the hook
  doesn't unscrew, thread the
  hook through the center point
  of the knitting.
With the right side of fabric
  facing and the cable strip
  sitting to the flat front part of
  hanger, wrap the fabric around
  the hanger—use safety pins to
  hold the back seam together.
Next, using mattress stitch, sew
  along the straight edges at the
  back of the coat hanger.
Sew the open side seams.
Once the hanger is covered, find
  the hole for the metal hook,
  push it through the fabric, and
  screw back into place.

MATERIALS

Rowan Handknit Cotton DK
(100% cotton, approx.
93 yd/85 m per ball)
1 x shade 251 Ecru

1 wooden coat hanger
approx. 16 in/40 cm
in length, 3½ in/9 cm
circumference

1 sheet beige felt fabric—long
enough to cover and wrap
around coat hanger

Double-sided sticky tape

EQUIPMENT

1 pair size US 6 (4 mm)
knitting needles

1 cable needle

Tapestry needle

Safety pins

GAUGE

Approx. 20 sts x 28 rows =
4 in (10 cm) in stockinette
stitch

tip
If your coat hanger is
thicker than the size
given, simply add
extra stitches to each
side of the cable.

knitted collar

This on-trend knitted collar is knitted in one piece from the top down; the shape is created with clever use of increasing and wrapping stitches.

Using size US 7 (4.5 mm) needles, cast on 81 sts.

Row 1 (WS): K2, purl to last 2 sts, K2.

Row 2: K3,* M1 by picking up the strand in between stitches and knitting into the back, K3, rep from * to end (107 sts).

Row 3: Repeat row 1.

Row 4: Knit to end.

Row 5: Repeat row 1.

Shape left-hand side of collar as follows:

Next row: K20, yo, slip next st, yarn back, turn.

Next row: Sl1, purl to last 2 sts, K2.

Next row: K16, yo, slip next st, yarn back, turn.

Next row: Sl1, purl to last 2 sts, K2.

Next row: K14, yo, slip next st, yarn back, turn.

Next row: Sl1, purl to last 2 sts, K2.

Next row: K12, yo, slip next st, yarn back, turn.

Next row: Sl1, purl to last 2 sts, K2.

Next row: K8, yo, slip next st, yarn back, turn.

Next row: Sl1, purl to last 2 sts, K2.

Next row: Knit to end, picking up wrapped stitches and working together.

Shape right-hand side of collar as follows:

Next row: K2, P18, yarn back, Sl1, yo, turn.

Next row: Sl1, knit to end.

Next row: K2, P14, yarn back, Sl1, yo, turn.

Next row: Sl1, knit to end.

Next row: K2, P12, yarn back, Sl1, yo, turn.

Next row: Sl1, knit to end.

Next row: K2, P10, yarn back, Sl1, yo, turn.

Next row: Sl1, knit to end.

Next row: K2, P6, yarn back, Sl1, yo, turn.

Next row: Sl1, knit to end.

Work across all stitches as follows:

Next row: K2, purl to last 2 sts, K2, picking up wrapped stitches and working together.

Next row: K2, K2togtbl, K2, yo, slip next st, yarn back, turn.

Next row: Sl1, P1, P2togtbl, K2, turn.

Knit across all stitches.

Next row: K2, P2tog, P2, yarn back, Sl1, yo, turn.

Next row: Sl1, K1, K2tog, K2.

Next row: K2, K2togtbl, knit to last 4 sts—picking up wrapped stitches and working together, K2tog, K2.

Knit across all stitches.

Bind off knitwise.

FINISHING

Weave in loose ends.

Block and press collar.

Place button at cast-on edge of collar and sew into place, then match up to the other side of collar and sew in small length of yarn to make a loop.

MATERIALS

Rowan All Seasons Cotton (60% cotton, 40% acrylic, approx. 98 yd/90 m per 1¾ oz/50 g ball)

1 x shade 178 Organic

1 shank button

EQUIPMENT

1 pair size US 7 (4.5 mm) knitting needles

Tapestry needle

GAUGE

Approx. 25 sts x 18 rows = 4 in (10 cm) in stockinette stitch

FINISHED SIZE

To fit average adult

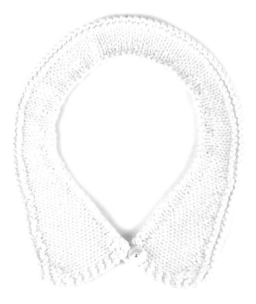

crossover scarf

This design will sit snugly around the neck—it crosses over to the front with one of the shaped ends slipping neatly into the double buttonhole opening at the other end of the scarf. Knit it using a super bulky wool—you will have enough yarn to make two from a 3½-oz (100-g) ball. You could also make the scarf longer by adding extra straight rows between the shaped ends.

MATERIALS

Rowan Big Wool (100% wool, approx. 88 yd/80 m per 3½ oz/100 g ball)
1 x shade 054 Vert

EQUIPMENT

1 pair size US 17 (12.5 mm) knitting needles

Tapestry needle

GAUGE

Approx. 8 sts x 11 rows = 4 in (10 cm) in stockinette stitch

FINISHED SIZE

To fit average adult

Using size US 17 (12 mm) needles, cast on 3 sts.

Row 1: Knit.

Row 2: Knit.

Row 3: K1, M1 by picking up the strand in between stitches and knitting into the back, K1, M1, K1 (5 sts).

Row 4: K2, P1, K2.

Row 5: K3, M1, K1, M1, K3 (7 sts).

Row 6: K2, P3, K2.

Row 7: K3, M1, K1, M1, K3 (9 sts).

Row 8: K2, P5, K2.

Row 9: K4, M1, K1, M1, K4 (11 sts).

Row 10: K2, P7, K2.

Row 11: K4, Sl2 knitwise, K1, psso, K4 (9 sts).

Row 12: Repeat row 8.

Row 13: K3, Sl2 knitwise, K1, psso, K3 (7 sts).

Row 14: Repeat row 6.

Row 15: K2, Sl2 knitwise, K1, psso, K2 (5 sts).

Row 16: Repeat row 4.

Row 17: Repeat row 5 (7 sts).

Row 18: K3, P1, K3.

Row 19: Knit to end.

Row 20: Repeat row 18.

Row 21: Repeat row 7 (9 sts).

Row 22: K4, P1, K4.

Row 23: Knit to end.

Row 24: Repeat row 22.

Row 25: Repeat row 9 (11 sts).

Row 26: K5, K1, K5.

Row 27: Knit to end.

Repeat the last 2 rows 10 more times.

Then repeat row 25 once more.

If you want to make scarf longer add extra rows here.

Make double buttonhole slit as
   follows:
Next row: K2, K2tog, turn.
Work on these 3 sts only.
Knit 4 rows—break off yarn and
   rejoin over next 3 sts.
Next row: K3.
Next row: K1, P1, K1.
Repeat last 2 rows once more
   and then K3 once more—
   break off yarn and rejoin over
   last 4 sts.
Next row: K2togtbl, K2.
Next row: Knit.
Knit 3 more rows.
Work across all 9 sts on needle.
Next row (WS): K4, P1, K4.
Next row: Repeat row 13 (7 sts).
Next row: K3, P1, K3.
Next row: Knit to end.
Next row: K3, P1, K3.
Next row: Repeat row 15 (5 sts).
Next row: K2, P1, K2.
Next row: Repeat row 5 (7 sts).
Next row: Repeat row 6.
Next row: Repeat row 7 (9 sts).
Next row: Repeat row 8.
Next row: Knit to end.
Repeat last 2 rows once more,
   then row 8 once more.
Next row: Repeat row 13 (7 sts).
Next row: Repeat row 6.
Next row: Repeat row 15 (5 sts).
Next row: Repeat row 4.
Next row: K1, Sl2, K1, psso, K1
   (3 sts).
Next row: Knit to end.
Next row: K3tog.
Break off yarn and thread
   through last st on needle.

ASSEMBLY
Weave in loose ends.
Block and press gently to flatten
   shaped ends.

string of birds

This decorative string of birds will brighten up any room; knitted in cheery shades, they will perch perfectly. Make the string as long or short as you want, mixing and matching combinations of colors.

Work front and back panel for each bird.

FRONT PANEL
Using size US 3 (3.25 mm) needles, cast on 5 sts.
Row 1 (WS): Purl to end.
Row 2: K1, M1 by picking up the strand in between sts and knitting into the back, K3, M1, K1 (7 sts).
Row 3: Purl to end.
Row 4: K1, M1, K5, M1, K1 (9 sts).
Row 5: Purl to end.
Row 6: K1, M1, K7, M1, K1 (11 sts).
Row 7: Purl to last st, M1, P1 (12 sts).
Row 8: K1, M1, K10, M1, K1 (14 sts).
Row 9: Repeat row 7 (15 sts).
Row 10: K1, M1, K13, M1, K1 (17 sts).
Row 11: Repeat row 7 (18 sts).

SHAPE HEAD
Next row: K7, yo, slip next st, yarn back, turn.
Next row: Sl1, P5, yarn back, Sl1, yo, turn.
Next row: Sl1, K4, yo, slip next st, yarn back, turn.

Next row: Sl1, P4, yarn back, Sl1, yo, turn.
Next row: Sl1, K2, yo, slip next st, yarn back, turn.
Next row: Sl1, P1, yarn back, Sl1, yo, turn.
Next row: Sl1, knit to end, picking up strand around wrapped stitch, slipping onto the left-hand needle, and working together with stitch.

WORK TAIL
Next row: P6, yarn back, Sl1, yo, turn.
Next row: Sl1, knit to end.
Next row: P4, yarn back, Sl1, yo, turn.
Next row: Sl1, knit to end.
Next row: P2, yarn back, Sl1, yo, turn.
Next row: Sl1, knit to end.
Next row: Purl to end, picking up strand around wrapped stitch, slipping onto the left-hand needle, and working together with stitch.
Do not bind off, place on spare needle.

BACK PANEL
Using size US 3 (3.25 mm) needles, cast on 5 sts.

MATERIALS

Rowan Cotton Glace (100% cotton, approx. 127 yd/116 m per 1¾ oz/50 g ball)
A shade 741 Poppy
B shade 844 Green slate
C shade 832 Persimmon
D shade 814 Shoot
E shade 841 Garnet

Toy stuffing

Sheets of felt fabric in the following colors:
BEAKS yellow
BIRD A tail—pink, wings—orange
BIRD B tail—green, wings—turquoise
BIRD C tail—ochre, wings—pink
BIRD D tail—bright yellow, wings—mid-green
BIRD E tail—pink, wings—lilac

Threads to match felt colors

2 small black beads per bird, for eyes

String to thread birds onto

31 glass beads

1 small bell

Spare needle

EQUIPMENT

1 pair size US 3 (3.25 mm) knitting needles
Pins
Tapestry needle
Sharp sewing needle

GAUGE

Approx. 25 sts x 32 rows = 4 in (10 cm) in stockinette stitch

TEMPLATE

See page 125

◄ projects

Row 1 (WS): Purl to end.

Row 2: K1, M1 by picking up the strand in between sts and knitting into the back, K3, M1, K1 (7 sts).

Row 3: Purl to end.

Row 4: K1, M1, K5, M1, K1 (9 sts).

Row 5: Purl to end.

Row 6: K1, M1, K7, M1, K1 (11 sts).

Row 7: P1, M1, purl to end (12 sts).

Row 8: K1, M1, K10, M1, K1 (14 sts).

Row 9: Repeat row 7 (15 sts).

Row 10: K1, M1, K13, M1, K1 (17 sts).

Row 11: Repeat row 7 (18 sts).

WORK TAIL

Next row: K6, yo, Sl1, yarn back, turn.

Next row: Sl1, purl to end.

Next row: K4, yo, Sl1, yarn back, turn.

Next row: Sl1, purl to end.

Next row: K2, yo, Sl1, yarn back, turn.

Next row: Sl1, purl to end.

Next row: Knit to end, picking up strand around wrapped stitch, slipping onto the left-hand needle, and working together with stitch.

SHAPE HEAD

Next row: P7, yarn back, Sl1, yo, turn.

Next row: Sl1, K4, yo, Sl1, yarn back, turn.

Next row: Sl1, P4, yarn back, Sl1, yo, turn.

Next row: Sl1, K3, yo, Sl1, yarn back, turn.

Next row: Sl1, P2, yarn back, Sl1, yo, turn.

Next row: Sl1, knit to end,

picking up strand around wrapped stitch, slipping onto the left-hand needle, and working together with stitch.

Next row: Purl to end, picking up strand around wrapped stitch, slipping onto the left-hand needle, and working together with stitch.

Bind off front and back panels together using the 3-needle bind-off method as follows:

Hold wrong sides together and insert needle through 1st st on both needles, then knit.

Repeat this for the 2nd st on needle.

Next pass 1st st over the top of second and pass off the needle.

Repeat this until all sts have been bound off.

Break off yarn and slip through last sts—pull tight.

ASSEMBLY

Gently press front and back panels.

Next sew front and back seams leaving the bottom edge open to insert stuffing.

Next insert stuffing; make sure stuffing goes into the head and tail sections.

Once you are happy with the amount of stuffing sew bottom edge.

BEAK

Cut a small square from yellow felt, approx. ½ in (1 cm).

Fold in half to form 2 triangles.

Then pin and stitch into position at front of head.

TAIL

Cut a length of felt fabric approx. 10 in (25 cm) long and

¼ in (0.5 cm) wide and, using picture as guide, fold to make approx. 4 loops.

Pin and stitch the loops together to keep them in position.

Next pin and stitch the loops to the top of the tail.

WINGS

Using the template, cut out wing shape from felt for each bird.

Pin into position on the bound-off edge at the top of the bird.

Stitch into position down center of the wings along the back.

EYES

Using picture as guide, sew 1 bead to either side of the head for eyes.

STRINGING THE BIRDS

Lay out the birds in the order that you want them to be.

Next lay out the glass beads in the order you want them to be placed between the birds.

Measure out the length of string you require—make it longer than you need as you can trim to the required length.

Starting at the bottom work your way up through the birds as follows:

Thread 3 beads, the bell, then 3 more beads onto the string.

Knot the string to form a loop with 3 beads on both sides and the bell at center bottom, then bring the needle threaded with the string up through the center of the bottom and out between the wings of the first bird.

Next thread 5 beads onto the string, and insert needle up through the next bird.

Repeat until all birds have been threaded together.

Add the final set of 5 beads to the top.

acorn

Bring a piece of Fall into your home with this acorn pattern. The pattern is created using a mix of knit and purl stitches to create the texture and with minimal increasing and decreasing to form the shape.

Using size US 3 (3.25 mm) needles, cast on 8 sts.

Row 1 (RS): Purl to end.

Row 2: K1,* M1 by picking up the strand in between stitches and knitting into the back, K1, rep from * to end (15 sts).

Starting with a purl row, work in stockinette stitch for 4 more rows.

Break off yarn A and join yarn C.

Starting with a knit row, work in stockinette stitch for 6 more rows.

Row 13: K1, * K2tog, rep from * to end (8 sts).

Break off yarn, leaving a long enough length to sew the side seam.

Thread stitches onto the loose end and pull tight.

Sew side seam down to the color change.

Insert stuffing into the top section.

Sew rest of seam, and then insert more stuffing.

Sew bottom opening.

STALK

Using yarn B and size US 3 (3.25 mm) needles, cast on 10 sts, then bind off knitwise.

Break off yarn, leaving 8 in (20 cm) to sew stalk to bottom of acorn.

Sew stalk to bottom of acorn and weave in the loose ends.

MATERIALS

Rowan Cotton Glace (100% cotton, approx. 126 yd/ 115 m per 1¾ oz/50 g ball)

A shade 843 Toffee
B shade 838 Umber

Rowan Siena 4-ply (100% cotton, approx. 153 yd/ 140 m per 1¾ oz/50 g ball)

C Siena 4-ply shade 659 Oak

Toy stuffing

EQUIPMENT

1 pair size US 3 (3.25 mm) knitting needles

Sewing up needle

tumbling leaves

Keep Fall alive all year round with these lovely tumbling leaf patterns. Each leaf is worked from the stalk up toward the tip. The shapes are created using a variety of increasing and decreasing techniques along with casting on and binding off to create the organic shapes.

leaf a *orange leaf*

STALK

Using yarn A and double-pointed needles, cast on 4 sts.

Knit to the end of the row—do not turn, slide the stitches back up to the right-hand point of the needle, insert needle in right hand into the 1st stitch, bring the yarn from the left-hand side, and knit to the end of the row.

Work 3 more rows of I-cord.

Next row: Still working as I-cord K1, K2tog, K1 (3 sts).

Work 6 more rows.

MAIN LEAF

Working from right to left with right side facing, for this row only, still bring the yarn around as if working I-cord.

Row 1: K1, M1, K1, M1, K1, turn and cast on 6 sts (11 sts).

Row 2: P11, turn and cast on 6 sts (17 sts).

Row 3: K6, K2togtbl, K1, K2tog, K5, M1, K1 (16 sts).

Row 4: Purl to last 2 sts, M1, P1 (17 sts).

Row 5: K6, K2togtbl, K1, K2tog, K6 (15 sts).

Row 6: Bind off 3 sts, purl to end (12 sts).

Row 7: Bind off 3 sts, knit to end (9 sts).

Row 8: Cast on 5 sts, purl to end (14 sts).

Row 9: Cast on 5 sts, knit to end (19 sts).

Row 10: Purl to end.

Row 11: K7, K2togtbl, K1, K2tog, K7 (17 sts).

Row 12: Purl to end.

Row 13: K6, K2togtbl, K1, K2tog, K6 (15 sts).

Row 14: Purl to end.

Row 15: Bind off 3 sts, knit to end (12 sts).

Row 16: Bind off 3 sts, purl to end (9 sts).

Row 17: Cast on 5 sts, knit to end (14 sts).

Row 18: Cast on 5 sts, purl to end (19 sts).

Repeat rows 11 to 16 once more.

SHAPE TOP

Next row: Knit to end.

Next row: Purl to end.

Next row: K3, Sl2, K1, psso, K3 (7 sts).

Next row: Purl to end.

Next row: K2, Sl2, K1, psso, K2 (5 sts).

Next row: Purl to end.

Next row: K1, Sl2, K1, psso, K1 (3 sts).

Next row: Purl to end.

Next row: K3tog.

Break off yarn.

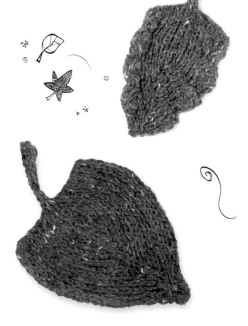

leaf b *pale green leaf*

Using size US 3 (3.25 mm) needles and yarn B, work stalk as given for leaf A.

MAIN LEAF

Working from right to left with right side facing, for this row only, still bring the yarn around as if working I-cord.

Row 1: K1, M1, K1, M1, K1 turn and cast on 6 sts (11 sts).

Row 2: P10, turn and cast on 6 sts (17 sts).

Row 3: Knit to end.

Row 4: Purl to end.

Row 5: K1, K4togtbl, knit to last 5 sts, K4tog, k1 (11 sts).

Row 6: Purl to end.

Row 7: K1, knit into the front and back of the next st twice, knit until 2 sts, knit into front and back of next stitch twice, K1 (17 sts).

Row 8: Purl to end.

Row 9: K1, M1, knit to last sts, M1, K1 (19 sts).

Row 10: Purl to end.

Row 11: K1, K4togtbl, knit to last 5 sts, K4tog, k1 (13 sts).

Row 12: Purl to end.

Row 13: K1, knit into the front and back of the next sts twice, K2, Sl2 knitwise, K1, psso, knit to last 2 sts, knit into the front and back of the next sts twice, K1 (17 sts).

Row 14: Purl to end.

Row 15: K7, Sl2 knitwise, K1, psso, knit to end (15 sts).

Row 16: Purl to end.

Row 17: K1, K4togtbl, knit to last 5 sts, K4tog, K1 (9 sts).

Row 18: Purl to end.

Row 19: K1, knit into the front and back of the next st twice, K1, Sl2 knitwise, K1, psso, K1,

knit into the front and back of the next st twice, K1 (13 sts).

Starting and ending with a purl row, work 3 rows stockinette stitch.

Row 23: K1, K3togtbl, K1, Sl2 knit wise, K1, psso, K1, K3tog, K1 (7 sts).

Row 24: Purl to end.

Row 25: K2, K1, Sl2 knitwise, K1, psso, K2 (5 sts).

Row 26: Purl to end.

Row 27: K1, Sl2 knitwise, K1, psso, K1 (3 sts).

Row 28: Purl.

Row 29: K3tog.

Break off yarn.

leaf c *dark green leaf*

Using size US 3 (3.25 mm) needles and yarn C, work stalk as given for leaf A.

MAIN LEAF

Row 1: K1, M1, K1, M1, K1 turn and cast on 9sts (14 sts).

Row 2: P14, turn and cast on 9sts (23 sts).

Row 3: Knit to end.

Row 4: Purl to end.

Row 5: K5, K2togtbl, K4, M1, K1, M1, K4, K2tog, K5 (23 sts).

Row 6: Purl to end.

Repeat the last 2 rows twice more.

Row 11: K10, Sl2 knit wise as if working K2tog, K1, psso, knit to end (21 sts).

Row 12 & every WS row purl to end.

Row 13: K9, Sl2, K1, psso, knit to end (19 sts).

Row 15: K8, Sl2, K1, psso, knit to end (17 sts).

Row 17: K7, Sl2, K1, psso, knit to end (15 sts).

Row 19: K6, Sl2, K1, psso, knit to end (13 sts).

Row 21: K5, Sl2, K1, psso, knit to end (11 sts).

Row 23: K1, K2togtbl, K1, Sl2, K1, psso, K1, K2tog, K1 (7 sts).

Row 25: K2, Sl2, K1, psso, knit to end (5 sts).

Row 27: K1, Sl2, K1, psso, knit to end (3 sts).

Break off yarn and thread through 3 sts on needle.

ASSEMBLY FOR ALL THE LEAVES

Weave in loose ends and block and press leaf to correct shape—use picture as guide.

LEAF A AND B

Using contrasting yarn and picture as guide, work a running stitch to create veins.

FINISHING OFF

Using knitted leaves as a guide, cut out shapes from gray felt fabric. Then pin into position on the wrong side of the knitted leaf. Next using sharp sewing needle and matching thread sew the backing onto the leaf.

dog bone key ring

This project is made from two knitted panels that are worked in stockinette stitch; the bone shape is created by simple increasing and decreasing techniques.

Front and back are both alike.
Using size US 3 (3.25 mm)
 needles, cast on 5 sts.
Row 1 (WS): Purl.
Row 2: K1, M1 by picking up the
 strand in between stitches and
 working into the back, K3, M1,
 K1 (7 sts).
Row 3: P1, M1, P5, M1, P1
 (9 sts).
Row 4: Knit to end.
Row 5: Purl to end.
Break off yarn and slip onto
 spare needle or stitch holder.
Repeat the last 5 rows—do not
 break off yarn.
Knit across 9 sts on needle, cast
 on 9 sts using 2-needle cast on
 method, then knit across
 9 sts on spare needle (27 sts).
Starting with a purl row, work
 3 rows in stockinette stitch.
Row 10: K1, K2tog tbl, knit to
 last 3 sts, K2tog, K1 (25 sts).
Row 11: P1, P2tog, purl to last
 3 sts, P2togtbl, P1 (23 sts).
Row 12: Repeat row 10 (21 sts).
Row 13: Purl to end.
Row 14: K1, M1, knit to last 2 sts,
 M1, K1 (23 sts).
Row 15: P1, M1, purl to last sts,
 M1, P1 (25 sts).
Row 16: Repeat row 14 (27 sts).
Starting with a purl row, work
 3 rows in stockinette stitch.
Row 20: K9, bind off 9 sts, knit
 to end.
Work on 1st set of 9 sts as
 follows:

Next row: Knit.
Next row: Purl.
Next row: P1, P2tog, P3,
 P2togtbl, P1 (7 sts).
Next row: K1, K2togtbl, K1,
 K2tog, K1 (5 sts).
Next row: Purl to end.
Bind off.
Rejoin to remaining 9 sts and
 work as given.
Work back panel to match.

ASSEMBLY

Weave in loose ends, then block
 and press.
With wrong sides together,
 sew the front and back panels
 together using mattress
 stitch—leave the top bound-
 off 9 sts open. Insert stuffing
 to make bone shape—do not
 overstuff. Once you are happy
 with the amount of stuffing,
 sew top opening.

STRAP

Using size US 2 (2.75 mm)
 needles, cast on 5 sts.
Row 1: K1, P1, K1, P1, K1.
Work 15 more rows as row 1.
Bind off.

FINISHING

Sew cast-on end of strap to
 center top of bone, slip the
 keyring onto strap, and then
 fold over and sew bound-off
 end to match.
Weave in loose ends.

MATERIALS

Rowan Pure Life Organic
Cotton DK (100% cotton,
approx. 131 yd/120 m per
1¾ oz/50 g ball)

1 x shade 989 Cherry plum

Thread

Toy stuffing

1 double-loop metal key ring

EQUIPMENT

1 pair size US 3 (3.25 mm)
knitting needles, plus one
spare needle

Spare needle or stitch holder

1 pair size US 2 (2.75 mm)
knitting needles

Tapestry needle

GAUGE

Approx. 25 sts x 32 rows
= 4 in (10 cm) in stockinette
stitch

dragonfly

This whimsical take on a dragonfly will make a great decoration or brooch. By using a contrasting wire-and-yarn combination the wings take on that characteristic iridescent look and will sparkle and catch the light.

MATERIALS

Rowan Cotton Glace (100% cotton, approx. 127 yd/ 116 m per 1¾ oz/50 g ball)
A shade 814 Shoot
B shade 849 Winsor
C shade 727 Black

Lime green 30-gauge (0.3 mm thick) craft wire

EQUIPMENT

1 pair size US 3 (3.25 mm) double-pointed needles

Tapestry needle

WINGS *make 2 sets*

With size US 3 (3.25 mm) needles, and using 1 strand of wire and 1 strand of yarn A, cast on 2 sts.
Row 1: Knit to end.
Row 2: Knit to end.
Row 3: K1, yo, K1 (3 sts).
Row 4: K1, Ktbl, K1.
Row 5: Knit to end.
Row 6: Knit to end.
Row 7: K1, yo, K2 (4 sts).
Row 8: K2, Ktbl, K1.
Work 10 more rows in garter stitch.
Row 19: K1, K2tog, K1 (3 sts).
Work 9 more rows in garter stitch.
Row 29: K1, yo, K2 (4 sts).
Row 30: K2, Ktbl, K1.
Work 10 more rows in garter stitch.
Row 41: K1, K2togtbl, K1 (3 sts).
Work 3 more rows in garter stitch.
Row 45: K1, K2tog (2 sts).
Row 46: Knit to end.
Bind off.
Make 2nd wing using 1 strand of wire and 1 strand of yarn B, cast on 2 sts.
Continue as first wing.

BODY

With US size 3 (3.25 mm) needles, and yarn C, cast on 3 sts, then work 14 rows as I-cord.
Row 15: K1, M1 by picking up strand between stitches and work into the back, K1, M1, K1 (5 sts).
Work 7 rows in garter stitch.
Row 23: K1, Sl1, K1, psso, K1 (3 sts).
Row 24: K1, Kfb into next stitch 3 times, turn.
Work on 6 sts just made only.
Work 4 rows in garter stitch.
Next row: Pass 5 sts of the 6 over the top of the 1st stitch and off the needle, K1 (3 sts).
Break off yarn and pull through.

ASSEMBLY

Next, using your fingers, flatten and open out the wing sections.
Then using picture as guide, pin and stitch into position on the body.

butterfly clip

Keep all your loose notes together in one place with this decorative butterfly clothespin clip. Each wing is worked separately, using brightly colored cotton yarn, and decorated with buttons, beads, and sequins.

The right and left sections are worked separately, creating the wing shapes using short row shaping technique, then stitched together to form butterfly shape.

WING 1

Using yarn A and size US 3 (3.25 mm) double-pointed needles, cast on 13 sts.
Row 1 (WS): Purl to end.
Work top section of wing as follows:
Next row: K6, yo, slip next st, yarn back, turn.
Next row: Sl1, purl to end.
Next row: K1, M1 by picking up the strand between the next 2 sts, K4, yo, slip next st, yarn back, turn.
Next row: Sl1, purl to end.
Next row: K1, M1, K3, yo, slip next st, yarn back, turn.
Next row: Sl1, purl to end.
Next row: K1, M1, K2, yo, slip next st, yarn back, turn.
Next row: Sl1, purl to end.
Next row: Knit across all stitches on the needle, picking up the strand around the wrapped stitches, slipping onto the needle, and working together.
Work bottom section of wing as follows:
Next row (WS): P4, yarn back, Sl1, yo, turn.

Next row: Sl1, K3, M1, K1, turn.
Repeat last two rows.
Break off yarn A and join yarn B.
Next row: Knit to end.
Next row: Knit to end.
Bind off knitwise.

WING 2

Using yarn A, cast on 13 sts.
Row 1 (WS): Purl to end.
Work bottom section of wing as follows:
Next row: K4, yo, slip next st, yarn back, turn.
Next row: Sl1, P3, M1, P1.
Repeat last 2 rows once more.
Knit across all stitches, picking up wraps and working them with stitches.
Work top section of wing as follows:
Next row (WS): P6, yarn back, Sl1, yo, turn.
Next row: Sl1, knit to end.
Next row: P1, M1, P4, yarn back, Sl1, yo, turn.
Next row: Sl1, knit to end.
Next row: P1, M1, P3, yarn back, Sl1, yo, turn.
Next row: Sl1, knit to end.
Next row: P1, M1, P2, yarn back, Sl1, yo, turn.
Next row: Sl1, knit to end.
Break off yarn A and join yarn B.
Next row: Knit to end.
Next row: Knit to end.
Bind off knitwise.

MATERIALS

Rowan Cotton Glace (100% cotton, approx. 126 yd/115 m per 1¾ oz/50 g ball)
A shade 841 Garnet
B shade 832 Persimmon
C shade 727 Black

1 reel 6-gauge (0.5 mm thick) craft wire

4 small glass beads

2 small buttons

2 flat sequins

1 wooden clothespin

EQUIPMENT

1 pair size US 3 (3.25 mm) double-pointed knitting needles

Tapestry needle

Pins

Double sided sticky tape or clear-drying craft glue

BODY

Using yarn C, cast on 3 sts, then work 10 rows as I-cord.

Row 11: K1, Kfb into next stitch twice then into the front once more, turn.

Work on 5 sts just made only.

Starting with a purl row, work 3 rows in stockinette stitch.

Next row: Pass 4 sts of the 5 over the top of the 1st stitch and off the needle, K1 (3 sts).

Next row: P3tog.

Break off yarn and pull through.

ASSEMBLY

Block and press wing sections, and then sew together along the cast-on edges leaving approx. 1 in (2.5 cm) free at each of the outer edges.

Weave in loose ends, place wings on body, then pin and stitch into place, using the picture as a guide.

FINISHING

ANTENNAE *make 2*

Cut length of wire approx. 8 in (20 cm) long, slide bead onto wire up toward the center, fold the wire in half, holding the bead between your thumb and finger, and twist to secure the bead in position.

Sew the non-beaded end of the wire into position on the head.

Attach the decorations to the wings—buttons to the larger top sections of wings and sequins with beaded centers to the smaller bottom sections of the wings.

Attach butterfly to clothespin using a strip of double-sided sticky tape or craft glue.

Aztec pot cover

Using the Fair Isle knitting technique worked in brightly colored Aztec-inspired worsted-weight cotton, this plant pot cover is designed to fit a medium-sized pot. The ribbed back will stretch to give a snug fit—if you want to make it larger simply add extra stitches to the ribbed section.

Using size US 6 (4 mm) needles and yarn A, cast on 49 sts.

The Fair Isle pattern is worked in between two 10-st 2 x 2 rib sections.

Row 1: K2, (P2, K2) twice, K39, K2, (P2, K2) twice.

Row 2: P2, (K2, P2) twice, P39, P2, (K2, P2) twice.

Keeping 2 x 2 rib section as set work from graph, ending with a knit row.

Bind off knitwise.

Break off yarn—leave long enough length to sew back seam.

ASSEMBLY

Weave in loose ends. Block and press Fair Isle section only.

Then using mattress stitch technique, sew back seam together.

MATERIALS

Rowan Handknit Cotton DK (100% cotton, approx. 93 yd/85 m per 1¾ oz/ 50g ball)

A shade 252 Black

B shade 215 Rosso

C shade 346 Atlantic

D shade 349 Ochre

E shade 251 Ecru

F shade 219 Gooseberry

EQUIPMENT

1 pair size US 6 (4 mm) knitting needles

Tapestry needle

GAUGE

Approx. 22 sts x 30 rows = 4 in (10 cm) in stockinette stitch

GRAPH

See page 123

equipment and techniques

All you really need to get started is a pair of knitting needles and some yarn, but as your skills progress you will find that you will need some additional equipment. It's a good idea to build up your knit kit as you go.

KNITTING NEEDLES— STRAIGHT

As the popularity of knitting has grown, so has the range of needles. The most common types are plastic, metal, bamboo, and birch wood. They come in different sizes—the larger the number, the thicker the needle.

The sizes quoted in the pattern instructions are a useful guide, but you might need to alter the size to achieve the correct fabric gauge. If your gauge is too slack the project will be too big and if it's too tight the result will be too small and will also use more yarn.

KNITTING NEEDLES— DOUBLE-POINTED

Double-pointed needles come in sets of four or five and are generally used for knitting smaller projects in the round, but can also be used to knit single-row stripes and for creating I-cords.

NEEDLE GAUGE

A needle gauge is very useful for checking or converting needle sizes, especially as the numbers printed on the needles can wear off with age.

CABLE NEEDLES

These short double-pointed needles are used to hold stitches at the front or back of the fabric when working cable patterns. They can be straight or U-shaped and come in various sizes. Always use a size that is smaller than the main needle you are knitting with.

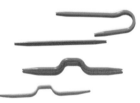

STITCH HOLDER

Stitch holders are used to hold stitches that you are not working with, rather than keeping them on your needles. If you are caught without a stitch holder you can always use a contrasting color of yarn—slip the yarn through the stitches and knot the ends together.

SAFETY PINS

A safety pin can be used as stitch holder if only a few stitches need to be held, or as a stitch marker if you don't have any to hand. They also come in handy if you need to catch a dropped stitch.

ROW COUNTER

A row counter fits neatly on the end of a knitting needle. Turn the dial as you work each row.

STITCH MARKER

Stitch markers are colored plastic or metal rings that are useful for marking stitches or rows. They are also very handy when you need to cast on a large number of stitches to help you keep count.

PINS

Glass-headed rustproof dressmaking pins are the best type to use. Plastic- or pearl-headed pins can be used unless heat is required (as the head of the pins will melt). It's also a good idea to use pins with brightly colored heads as they are easy to see against the fabric and if you drop them.

TAPE MEASURE/RULER

Choose a tape measure that shows both inches and centimeters on the same side; it's also a good idea to replace your tape measure if it's old and frayed as it is likely to have stretched, making it inaccurate. A clear plastic ruler is also good to have in your craft kit, for marking out shapes or lines on your fabric.

SCISSORS AND PLIERS

Scissors are an essential part of the kit; they are used in lots of different projects throughout the book. It is best to have several pairs for different uses: a small, sharp pair for cutting embroidery threads, a larger dressmaking pair for cutting fabrics, and a basic craft pair reserved for cutting out templates or fine craft wire—this type of cutting would blunt dressmaking scissors.

The most useful pliers are round-nose pliers, which have a cutting edge and a long, rounded nose. The nose has a textured inside surface for gripping.

NOTEBOOK

A notebook is essential but can often be overlooked. Use it to jot down any changes or adaptations to designs; if you scribble these down on loose scraps of paper they may get misplaced.

SEWING NEEDLES

There are many types of needles, each of which is designed for a different purpose. A tapestry needle has a blunt point and a large eye, and is used for weaving in ends of yarn. Sewing needles are used with thread to attach projects to backing fabric or to sew on embellishments such as buttons. You will need an embroidery needle to add embroidered embellishments—this type of needle has a long, thin eye and the head of the needle is usually narrow and flat, allowing it to move through the fabric easily.

reading a pattern

There is certain information contained in every written pattern, and it is important that you read through the entire pattern before starting to knit any project to ensure that you understand all of the abbreviations. Yarn amounts, needle sizes, and any extra equipment and materials will also appear at the beginning of a pattern.

abbreviations

The patterns in this book feature a number of standard abbreviations, which are explained below.

alt	alternate	LHN	left-hand needle	RS	right side
beg	begin(s)/beginning	lp(s)	loop(s)	RSF	right side facing
B1	bead 1	M1	make 1 stitch	sk	skip
BO	bind off	M1 p-st	make 1 stitch purlwise	sl	slip
CC	contrasting color	MC	main color	sl1k	slip one knitwise
cm	centimeter(s)	mm	millimeters	sl1p	slip one purlwise
cn	cable needle	p	purl	sl st	slip stitch
cont	continue	patt	pattern(s)	ssk	slip, slip, knit these 2 stitches together—a decrease
CO	cast on	psso	pass slipped stitch over		
dec	decrease(s)/ decreasing	p2sso	pass 2 slipped sts over	st(s)	stitch(es)
		p2tog	purl 2 stitches together	St st	stockinette stitch
DPN(s)	double-pointed needle(s)	pm	place marker	tbl	through back loop
foll	follow(s)/following	prev	previous	tog	together
in	inch(es)	pwise	purlwise	WS	wrong side
inc	increase(s)/increasing	rem	remain/remaining	yfwd	yarn forward
k	knit	rep	repeat(s)	yo	yarn over
k2tog	knit two stitches	rev St st	reverse stockinette stitch	yon	yarn over needle
kfb or K1f&b	knit into front and back of stitch	RH	right hand	yrn	yarn around needle
kwise	knitwise	RHN	right-hand needle	*	repeat from starting point (i.e., repeat from *)
LH	left hand	rnd(s)	round(s)		

gauge

Most knitting patterns specify an ideal gauge, which is the number of stitches and rows counted over a certain measurement, usually 4 in (10 cm) square. If your gauge is not correct, the knitting will end up the wrong size. This is not important for some projects, but it is crucial to get the gauge right when knitting something that is going to be worn, such as a hat or gloves.

MAKING A TEST SWATCH

Cast on the number of stitches given in the gauge guide plus four more. If the stitches are to be measured over a pattern, cast on the correct multiple of stitches to knit the pattern. Work in the required pattern until swatch measures approx. 5 in (12 cm). Then break off the yarn, slip it through the stitches, then slip off the needle—you don't have to bind off, as this can distort the stitches.

COUNTING STITCHES AND ROWS

Lay the swatch down on a flat surface, and in the center place a ruler horizontally on the square. Place a pin at one point and another 4 in (10 cm) away. Count the stitches between the pins; include the half stitches. Repeat the process vertically to count the rows. Remember to count accurately as even half a stitch could make a difference to the finished size.

ADJUSTING GAUGE

If you have fewer stitches than given your knitting is too loose and the garment will be too big. Knit up another swatch but using a smaller needle.

If you have more stitches than given your knitting is too tight and the garment will be too small. Knit up another swatch but using a bigger needle.

making a slipknot

A knitted fabric is made by working rows of stitches in various sequences. In order to create a fabric, you must first make a base row, known as a cast-on row. A slipknot is used as the first stitch for a cast-on row.

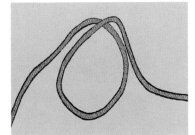

1 Holding the yarn in both hands, make a small loop in the yarn. Take the piece that you are holding in the right hand underneath the loop.

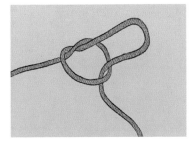

2 Pull this piece of yarn through the original loop, to create a knot. Do not pull the short end of the yarn through the loop.

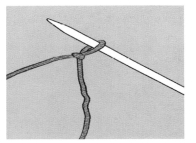

3 Place the slip knot onto the knitting needle.

casting on

Casting on is the first step in hand knitting and it provides the first row of loops on the needle. Different methods of casting on produce different types of edges. The diagrams below show the cable method, but if you are familiar with another method you can use that instead.

the cable method

This cast-on method uses both knitting needles and creates a strong edge with a double thickness of yarn. You do not need to allow for a tail end of yarn—the ball end of the yarn is held in the right hand, but the tail end of the yarn is not used and therefore can be short.

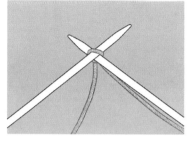

1 Place the slip knot onto the knitting needle and hold the needle in your left hand. Slide the right knitting needle through the loop created by the slip knot from front to back.

2 With your right hand, wrap the yarn around the right knitting needle counterclockwise from back to front.

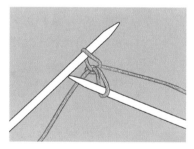

3 Slide the right needle through the loop on the left needle, catching the wrapped yarn and bringing it through the loop to create another loop.

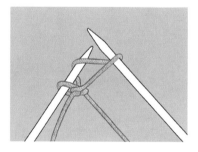

4 Pass the left needle over the top of the new loop, placing the tip of the needle through the loop on the right needle. Remove the right needle, thus transferring the stitch to the left needle.

5 Make each subsequent stitch by placing the right needle between the last two stitches made on the left needle, and repeating steps 2 through 4.

binding off

There is one simple and commonly used method of securing stitches once you have finished a piece of knitting: binding off. The most common—the cable bind-off—is shown below. These diagrams show binding off along a knit row. However, you can bind off in pattern along any fabric, simply working each stitch as set in pattern, instead of knitting all stitches across the row.

cable bind-off

Cable bind-off is a neat and tidy way of securing all the stitches so that they do not slip out of the last row worked. You achieve a cable bind-off using the two needles you have been knitting with all along.

1 At the point where you are ready to bind off, knit the first two stitches.

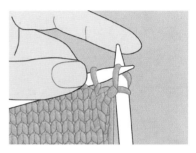

2 Slip the left-hand needle into the first stitch on the right-hand needle, and lift it over the second stitch and off the needle.

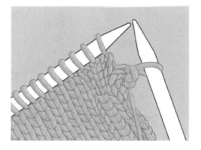

3 Knit next stitch so that there are two stitches on the right-hand needle again.

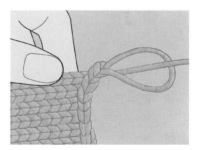

4 Repeat steps 2 and 3 until all stitches are knitted from the left-hand needle and one stitch remains on the right-hand needle. Make the last stitch loop larger, break the yarn and draw firmly through the last stitch to fasten off.

knit and purl

Most knitting is based on combinations of just two basic stitches—knit stitch and purl stitch. Once you have mastered these two stitches, you can work many different stitch patterns. The knit stitch is the simplest of all stitches. Knitting every row forms the ridged fabric called garter stitch. When you use purl in a fabric, you never work every row purl, as this fabric would look exactly the same as garter stitch. You usually work a row of purls followed by a row of knits, then alternate knit and purl every row, which is called stockinette stitch.

KNIT

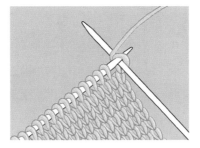

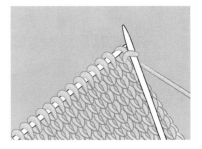

1 Hold the needle with the stitches to be knitted in the left hand with the yarn behind the work.

2 Insert the right-hand needle into a stitch from front to back. Take the yarn over it, forming a loop.

3 Bring the needle and the new loop to the front of the work through the stitch, and then slide the original stitch off the left-hand needle.

PURL

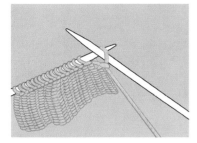

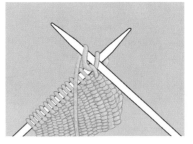

1 Hold the needle with the stitches to be purled in the left hand, with the yarn at the front of the work.

2 Insert the right-hand needle through the front of the stitch, from right to left. Take the yarn over and under, forming a loop.

3 Take the needle and the new loop through the back and slide the original stitch off the left-hand needle.

ribbing

A knit rib is simply a mix of knits and purls across a row. A rib can be any mix of knits and purls built up on top of each other in vertical lines or "ribs." A ribbed fabric is very stretchy and is therefore great in areas such as cuffs, where the fabric needs to grip more tightly to the body.

In order to work a ribbed pattern it is important that you change from a knit to a purl stitch and vice versa in the correct way.

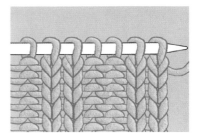

CHANGING FROM A PURL STITCH TO A KNIT STITCH

Having completed a purl stitch, the yarn will be held at the front of the work. In order to work a subsequent knit stitch, take the yarn to the back of the work between both knitting needles. Then knit the next stitch.

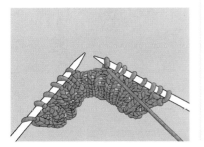

CHANGING FROM A KNIT STITCH TO A PURL STITCH

Having completed a knit stitch, the yarn will be held at the back of the work. In order to work a purl stitch, bring the yarn through to the front of the work between both knitting needles, then purl the next stitch.

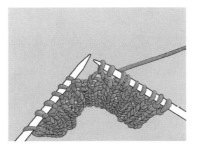

PRACTICE THIS

All knitting uses a combination of knit and purl stitches. The following projects are great for practicing switching between knit and purl stitches in the same row:

1 egg cozy *page 13*
2 mug cozy *page 15*
3 potholder *page 18*
4 baby pixie hat *page 29*
5 rib lace pompom hat *page 37*
6 arm warmers *page 42*
7 fingerless gloves *page 45*

shaping techniques—increasing

Shaping techniques are used to create shapes in a piece of knitting. Increasing techniques are used to make the fabric wider by adding to the number of stitches. The two most common ways of increasing are Make 1 (M1), which creates an increase between two stitches, and increasing by knitting into the front and back of a stitch (Inc), which is best worked at the beginning or end of the knitted piece. Both increasing and decreasing techniques are usually worked at least one stitch in from the edge to make sewing up and picking up stitches easier.

M1—MAKE 1

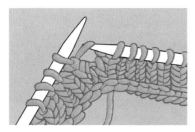

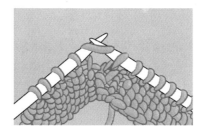

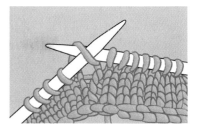

1 Insert the tip of the right-hand needle from front to back beneath the horizontal bar of yarn between two stitches where you want the increase.

2 Slip the bar onto the left-hand needle.

3 Create the new stitch by knitting through the back of the loop. This twists the loop and avoids making a hole.

INC—K1F&B OR KFB

This usually means knitting into the front and then the back of a stitch. This increase is best worked at either the beginning or end of the knitted piece, as it is not very neat.

1 Work to where the extra stitch is needed. Knit into the front of the next stitch on the left knitting needle without slipping it off.

2 With the stitch still on the left needle and the yarn at the back, knit into the back of the same stitch and slip it from the needle.

shaping techniques—decreasing

Decreasing techniques are used to make the fabric narrower by reducing the number of stitches. Various techniques are used, depending on whether the decrease needs to slope to the left or the right.

sloping to the right

K2TOG—KNIT 2 TOGETHER

To decrease a stitch knitwise, insert the needle from left to right through the first 2 stitches on the left-hand needle. Then knit as you would normally, slipping both stitches off the needle at the same time.

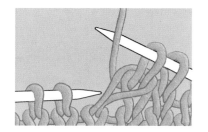 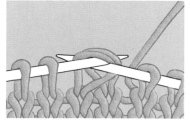

P2TOG—PURL 2 TOGETHER

To decrease a stitch purlwise, insert the needle from right to left through the first 2 stitches on the left-hand needle. Then purl as you would normally, slipping both stitches off the needle at the same time.

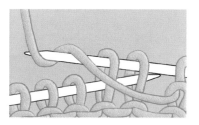 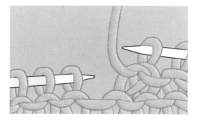

sloping to the left

SSK—SLIP, SLIP, KNIT

 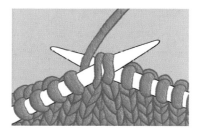 

1 To decrease knitwise, slip 2 stitches from the left-hand needle to the right-hand needle.

2 Insert the tip of the left-hand needle from left to right through the front loop of both stitches.

3 Knit them together from this position.

SSP—SLIP, SLIP, PURL

To decrease purlwise with this method, slip 2 purl stitches one at a time, from the left-hand needle to the right-hand needle. Slip both stitches back onto the left-hand needle purlwise. Purl both together through the back loop.

SKPO—SLIP, KNIT, PASS SLIPPED STITCH OVER

With this method of decrease, slip the first stitch from the left-hand to the right-hand needle without working it. Knit the next stitch as normal, and then pass the slipped stitch over and off the needle.

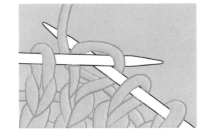 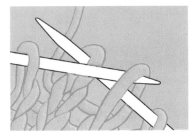

K2TOGTBL—KNIT 2 TOGETHER THROUGH BACK LOOP

To decrease a stitch knitwise, insert the needle from right to left through the back loop of the first 2 stitches on the left-hand needle. Then knit as you would normally, slipping both stitches off the needle at the same time.

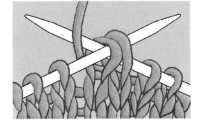

PRACTICE THIS

Many of the projects in this book use shaping techniques. Here are some simple ones that will help you gain confidence:

chick *page 11*
egg *page 12*
fish *page 14*
coasters *page 17*
little birds *page 21*
strawberry beanie *page 30*
bow hairpins *page 60*
crown *page 61*
bunting *page 67*

P2TOGTBL—PURL 2 TOGETHER THROUGH THE BACK LOOP

To decrease a stitch purlwise, insert the right-hand needle from left to right through the back loop of the first 2 stitches on the left needle. Then purl as you would normally, slipping both stitches off the needle at the same time.

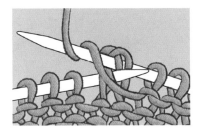

picking up stitches

Some knitting patterns will ask you to pick up stitches along either a horizontal or vertical edge. Stitches must be picked up evenly along the required edge using a knitting needle and yarn to create the stitches you will work into.

HORIZONTAL EDGE

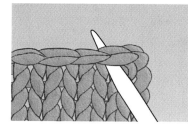
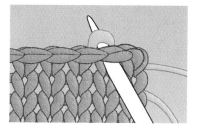
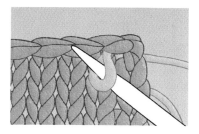

1 When picking up stitches along a bound-off or cast-on row, work into 1 full stitch above or below to give a neater finish. Holding the needle in your right hand insert the tip into the center of the first full stitch from the front to the back.

2 Next wrap the yarn around the needle as if you were working a knit stitch.

3 Then pull the loop on the needle through to the front of the fabric to create a new stitch. Complete this until you have the required number of stitches.

VERTICAL EDGE

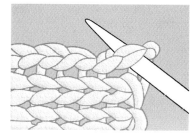

1 When picking up along an edge work 1 full stitch in from the edge. Holding the needle in your right hand insert the tip in between the first and second stitches from the front to the back.

2 Next wrap the yarn around the needle as if you were working a knit stitch, and then pull the loop on the needle through to the front of the fabric to create a new stitch. Complete this until you have the required amount of stitches.

cabling

A cable is made by crossing one set of stitches over another. Cables can cross to the left or the right. To work a cable you will need a cable needle to hold the stitches that you want to move either to the front or the back of the work, depending on the direction of the cable.

RIGHT CROSS CABLE

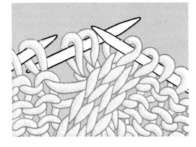

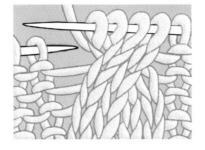

1 Slip the specified number of stitches off the left-hand needle and onto the cable needle. Hold the needle to the back of the work, and then work the specified number of stitches on the left-hand needle.

2 Next work the stitches on the cable needle, and then complete the row as required.

LEFT CROSS CABLE

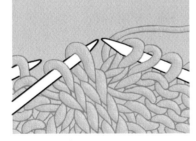

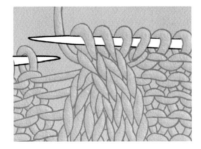

1 Slip the specified number of stitches off the left-hand needle and onto the cable needle. Hold the needle to the front of the work, and then work the specified number of stitches on the left-hand needle.

2 Next work the stitches on the cable needle, and then complete the row as required.

PRACTICE THIS

Cable knitting is used in the following projects:

egg cozy *page 13*
mug cozy *page 15*
ear warmer *page 41*
cable coat hanger *page 88*

color work

The projects in this book use a variety of different techniques for joining colors together—the two most important methods to know about are Fair Isle and intarsia.

fair isle

Fair Isle is the name given to a knitting technique where you use two colors repeatedly across a row to create a pattern. The Fair Isle technique is worked throughout in stockinette stitch so you end up with a right and a wrong side. These days most Fair Isle patterns are worked from a graph.

WORKING FROM A GRAPH
Graphs are read from the bottom up. Each square represents a stitch.

Right to left—knit row (odd numbers). Left to right—purl row (even numbers). The background shade is the main shade and the second color is the contrast—you work them in turn across the row according to the graph.

Simply float the color you are not working across the back of the fabric (right, top). If you have to carry the color over more than three stitches it is advisable to twist the strands along the back as this will help to give an even gauge (right, bottom).

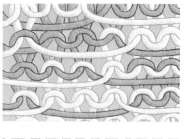

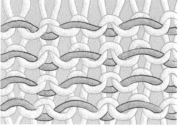

intarsia

Intarsia is the name given to color knitting where the pattern is worked in large blocks or over larger areas at a time, using separate balls of yarn for each color area. There can be any number of colors across a row, but because of the size of each color section the spare yarns should NOT be stranded across the back of the work. Generally intarsia knitting is worked in stockinette stitch and is used for large geometric patterns, patchworks, picture knitting, or individual motifs. Patterns are usually given in chart form— sometimes a complete section of a garment is shown if the pattern is large and non-repetitive.

TWISTING YARNS
An important point to remember about intarsia knitting is always to twist the two yarns when changing color. The yarns must be twisted over each other to link them together and prevent a hole from forming between the colors.

Always cross the yarns on the wrong side of the work, even if the garment is in reverse stockinette stitch.

Before you can get started knitting your intarsia pattern you must make small bobbins or balls in each required color; if you simply leave

all the skeins in your knitting basket you will end up with a knotted mess of yarn that will be very difficult to detangle later.

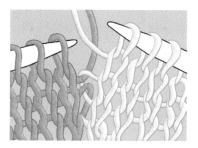

right: twisting yarns on a knit stitch

beaded knitting

Adding beads to your knitted fabric is a great way of adding color, texture, and patterning. It looks a lot more complicated than it actually is.

THREADING THE BEADS ONTO THE YARN

Thread a sewing needle with a small piece of sewing thread; tie the thread into a knot to form a loop.

Place the yarn into the loop, then thread the beads down the needle and then down onto the yarn. Alternatively, wrap a small twist of very fine wire around the yarn (see below) and thread the beads onto the wire.

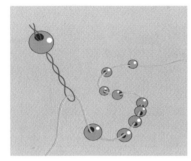

PLACING A BEAD—B1

Beaded knitting patterns can be written as a graph or as an ordinary pattern with the abbreviation B1 (bead 1).

Knit to the place where the bead is required. Bring the yarn forward between the needles, slip a bead up toward the needle, and then slip the next st on the left-hand needle purlwise onto the right-hand needle. Next, bring the yarn to the back of the work into position for working the next knit stitch.

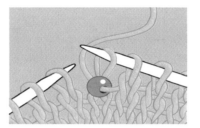

PRACTICE THIS

These projects use beaded knitting techniques:

lampshade decoration
page 49
beaded bow hairpins
page 60
strawberry charm *page 86*

I-cord

The I-cord is a tube knitted on the round with two double-pointed needles; it is a quick and easy way of making a versatile cord.

To work a cord successfully, cast on up to 3–5 stitches.

Knit to the end of the row—do not turn, slide the stitches back up to the right-hand point of the needle, insert needle in right hand into the first stitch, bring the yarn from the left-hand side and knit to the end of the row.

Keep repeating this process until the required length of cord is achieved. Bind off as you would normally, or thread the end of yarn through all the stitches on the needle and pull tight.

twisted cord

A twisted cord is a simple way of making a cord or strap for a knitted project. They can be made to any length or thickness.

TWISTED CORD

To make a twisted cord you will need to measure a length of yarn approximately 4 times longer than you want the finished length to be.

Once you have measured your length of yarn, bring the cut ends together and make a slipknot. Next place the slipknot onto a door handle and stand far enough away so that the yarn is pulled tightly and forms a straight line from you to the door handle.

Next put a pen or pencil into the loop, hold the yarn with your left hand and twirl the pencil around with the other to make the lengths of yarn twist around each other.

Once it is nice and taught, keeping hold of the pencil, pinch the yarn at the middle and bring the ends together by moving toward the door knob. It is important NOT to let go of the middle until both ends are together.

Remove the slipknot from the door handle, and holding both ends in one hand, let go of the middle and allow the cord to twist up on itself, you might need to run your hand down the cord to even out any kinks. Knot the open ends together.

blocking and pressing

Blocking and pressing finished work gives it a really professional finish, and is essential for a good result.

Arrange the pieces wrong side up on a padded surface. Place pins at frequent intervals around the very edges of the knitting into the padded surface, avoiding any ribs.

Check that the measurements are correct and that the lines of the stitches are straight in both the horizontal and vertical directions. Re-pin as necessary to achieve the correct size and shape, stretching or easing slightly if required so that the outline forms a smooth edge between the pins.

Depending on the fiber content of the yarn and the type of fabric you have used there are slightly different methods for blocking and pressing.

Natural fibers: Wool, cotton, linen, soya, hemp, bamboo (check these yarns do not have a high acrylic content)—place a damp cloth over the knitting and press gently with an iron, then remove the cloth and let dry before unpinning.

Synthetic fibers: Acrylic, polyester— DO NOT PRESS! Use damp finish technique: Lay pieces on a damp (colorfast) towel, then roll them up together and leave for about half an hour to let the knitting absorb moisture from the towel. Unwrap, lay the damp towel on a flat surface, and place the pieces on top. Ease the pieces into shape and pin as explained in the blocking section. Lay another damp towel over the top, pat firmly to establish contact, and let dry.

correcting mistakes

If you are a beginner, it is inevitable that you will make mistakes when knitting; even experts cannot fully avoid this. However, mistakes are as easy to fix as they are to make.

To rectify dropped stitches, keep a small crochet hook with you as you knit, and hook each missed strand through the loop of the dropped stitch. While it is often assumed that it is more common to lose stitches, it is actually easier to gain them. To avoid this, try to count your stitches every row as you practice, to see if you can spot where the mistake has been made. Watch that you do not pass the yarn from front to back when it is not called for, knit into only the stitch on the needle, not into the stitch below, do not wrap the yarn twice around the needle when knitting, and always try to remember to drop off the final loop at the end of a stitch. When ribbing, remember to always move between the front and back of the work when you are working a mixture of knits and purls.

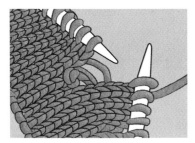

1 This shows what a dropped stitch looks like. If left, it will drop further to form a ladder. If this occurs, you must pick up each strand of the ladder, lowest first, to account for each row.

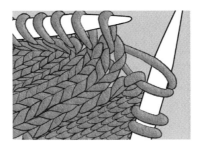

2 First, slip the dropped stitch loop on to the left needle. Pick up the strand of yarn from the ladder with right-hand needle.

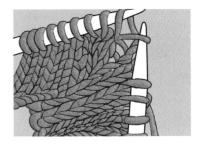

3 Slip the dropped loop from the left needle onto the right needle. Finally, slip the strand of yarn over the loop and off the end of the right-hand needle, as if binding off. Continue in this way until all the strands are picked up, from top to bottom.

finishing techniques

A great piece of knitting can be easily spoiled by the way it is sewn up. It seems a pity that many projects are ruined because so little care is taken in the finishing. It is worth learning these basic sewing techniques as they will make all the difference to your finished work.

JOINING BOUND-OFF EDGES
Two bound-off edges can be joined together using a mattress stitch technique so that the seam is matched exactly stitch for stitch.

Lay pieces flat with bound-off edges to the center. Working with the right sides facing, zigzag between the two pieces, going under the V that is directly above and below the bound-off edge.

JOINING SIDE ROWS
TO ROWS
This seam is also known as mattress stitch or ladder stitch. It is the seam that professionals use wherever possible. This stitch should be worked either one full stitch or half a stitch in from the edge, depending on the thickness of the fabric. You are always working with the right side facing, which allows you to match up patterns and shaping marks.

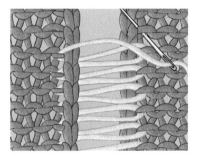

1 Place the two pieces flat and edge to edge. Thread needle and insert between the edge stitch and the second stitch of the first row—leave a long tail as this will be used to secure the bottom edge, or if you make a mistake it can be easily pulled out. Pass the needle under two rows, and then bring it back through to the front. Return to the opposite side and working under two rows at a time throughout repeat this zigzag action—always go back into the same space you came out of and make sure you match up any patterns or markings.

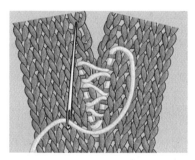

2 Work for approx. 2 in (5 cm) before pulling thread tight, stretch the seam slightly to give the required amount of elasticity, and continue with the next section of the seam.

charts

□ shade A
● shade B

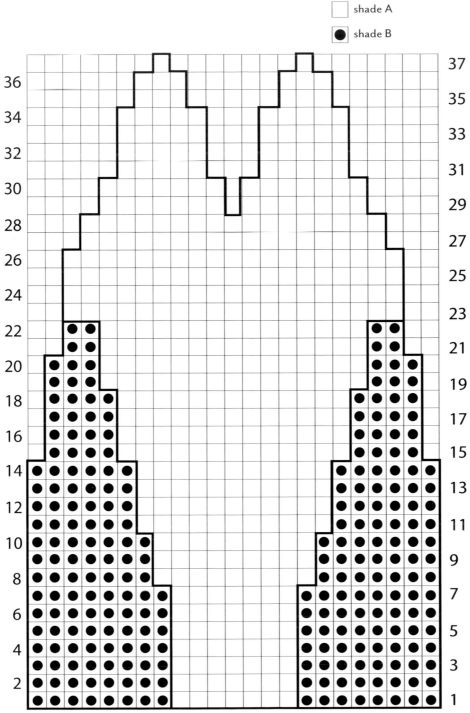

small cat pillow *page 68*
chart for color only

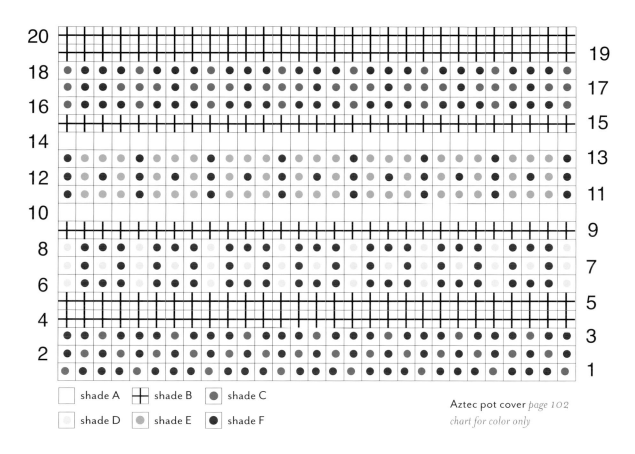

☐ shade A	✛ shade B	● shade C
◉ shade D	◉ shade E	● shade F

Aztec pot cover *page 102*
chart for color only

templates

apple pincushion *page 22*
template shown at actual size

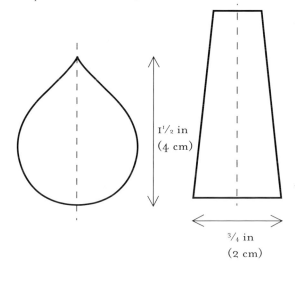

1½ in
(4 cm)

2 in
(5 cm)

¾ in
(2 cm)

phone cover *page 26*
increase template by 50%

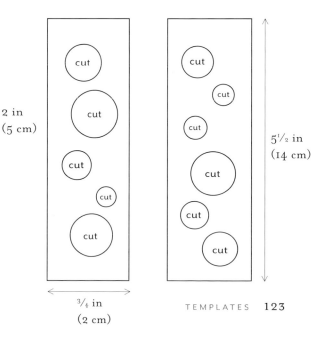

cut

cut

cut

cut

cut

cut

cut

cut

cut

cut

cut

5½ in
(14 cm)

¾ in
(2 cm)

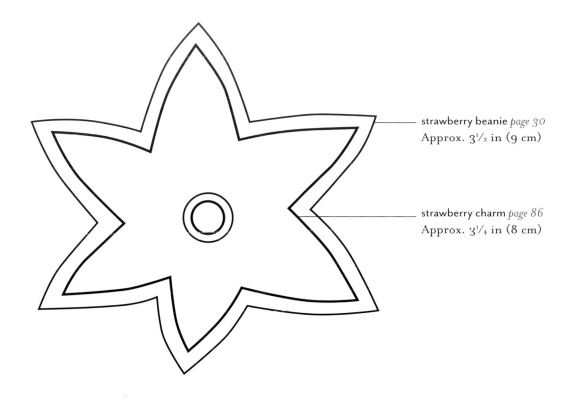

strawberry beanie *page 30*
Approx. $3^{1}/_{2}$ in (9 cm)

strawberry charm *page 86*
Approx. $3^{1}/_{4}$ in (8 cm)

ladybug key ring *page 38*
template shown at actual size

bumblebee key ring *page 39*
template shown at actual size

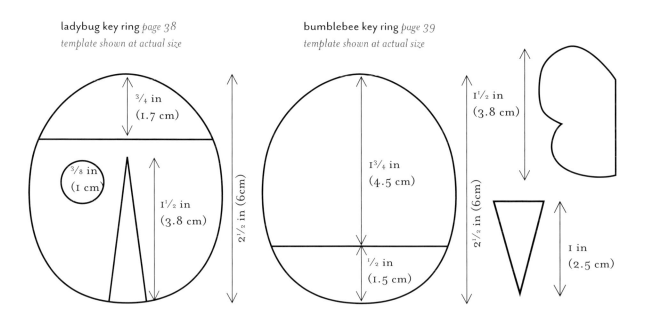

$^{3}/_{4}$ in (1.7 cm)

$^{3}/_{8}$ in (1 cm)

$1^{1}/_{2}$ in (3.8 cm)

$2^{1}/_{2}$ in (6cm)

$1^{3}/_{4}$ in (4.5 cm)

$^{1}/_{2}$ in (1.5 cm)

$2^{1}/_{2}$ in (6cm)

$1^{1}/_{2}$ in (3.8 cm)

1 in (2.5 cm)

small cat pillow *page 68*
increase template by 50%

8³⁄₄ in
(22cm)

6³⁄₄ in (17 cm)

Venetian mask *page 79*
increase template by 50%

FOLD HERE

sheep fridge magnet *page 72*
template shown at actual size

head

body

tail

leg

leaf headband *page 80*
template shown at actual size

2³⁄₄ in
(7 cm)

string of birds *page 93*
template shown at actual size

³⁄₈ in
(1 cm)

1¹⁄₄ in
(3.2 cm)

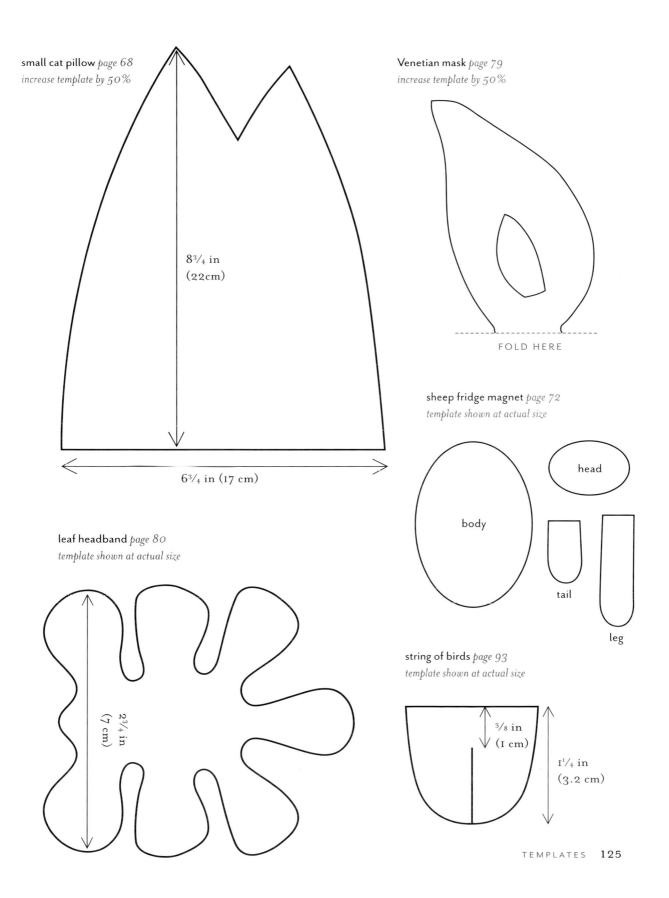

index

acknowledgments

Carol Meldrum: I would like to thank everybody for their help and support creating this fantastic book. Rowan and Coats Crafts UK for supplying the lovely materials used throughout the projects. My ever so patient and loving partner Andy Daly for supplying me with constant care and attention throughout. Thank you—I couldn't have done this without you all!

Quintet Publishing would also like to thank: the models Rai Quartley, Halla Vilhjálmsdóttir, and Isabelle Hissey; Jane Cumberbatch for the photography location; and The White Company for the Nantucket Cot Bed seen on page 66 (www.thewhitecompany.com).

All the projects in this book have been tested by a team of amateur knitters. Thanks to Sallie Chester, Liz Gregory, Maureen Johnson, Catherine McGregor, Kali Noble, and Carmel Searle for their help.